C000230517

Janet Morley is a freelance writer, speaker and workshop leader. She has worked for Christian Aid and for the Methodist Church. She is the author of several books of prayers and poems, including *All Desires Known*, *Bread of Tomorrow*, *The Heart's Time*, *Haphazard by Starlight* and *Our Last Awakening*, all published by SPCK.

Janet Morley

Love Set You Going

Poems of the heart

spck

First published in Great Britain in 2019

Society for Promoting Christian Knowledge
36 Causton Street
London SW1P 4ST
www.spck.org.uk

British Library Cataloguing-in-Publication Data
A catalogue record for this book is available from the British Library

ISBN 978–0–281–07892–9

1 3 5 7 9 10 8 6 4 2

Typeset by Fakenham Prepress Solutions, Fakenham, Norfolk NR21 8NL
Printed in Great Britain by TJ International

Produced on paper from sustainable forests

For Nicky

Contents

Contents

GROWN-UP LOVE

Contents

Contents

GOD AND THE HUMAN HEART

Contents

Love set you going

'Love set you going.' The opening words of Sylvia Plath's poem for her newborn daughter are true of us all. Love is fundamental to our being, our growth, development and continued well-being. It is that intimate sense of connection which shapes our human understanding and identity, impelling us to respond to another: to desire, protect or imitate, or somehow allow ourselves to be truly shaped by their presence. Love calls for sacrifice, and makes us willing to give it, surrendering our needs to those of another. It transforms our priorities and influences the direction of our lives more than any other human impulse we experience.

Though it is always quite specific, and tied to a particular person, love is never just one simple thing. It experiences stages of growth, reversal (and sometimes decay); it includes anxiety, ambivalence and surprise. It can be passionate, or lonely: light-hearted, or demanding. It is the source of our selves, and our capacity to grow and learn. It is the most important of connections between people, and it is the touchstone of how human beings relate to God. Love enables us to make meaning of our lives in the world and gives us hope for what lies beyond. It is completely humdrum and ordinary; it is mysterious beyond speech. It begins in the body, but it points us to eternity.

It may be worth asking why we should study poetry in order to reflect on love. In a way the answer seems obvious, as there is such a classic identification between the theme and the genre: giving love poems is one of the traditional techniques for advancing a romantic relationship. But I think the matter is more subtle. Praise (or even flattery) of the beloved may be persuasive, but what makes poems of the heart powerful is their honesty and accuracy about love. Poets notice things, and tend to focus on detail in a way that illuminates the theme and calls forth recognition and insight in the reader. This can include a refreshing acknowledgement of their own flaws, ambivalences, fantasies and fears, as well as the strength of their passions. It can also examine not just what love feels like but what it actually does.

There are a vast number of anthologies of love poems, but most of them seem to focus exclusively on the kind of love that is associated with erotic passion, the experience of falling in love between adults who are seeking a partner. But life offers us, and asks of us, many different kinds of love, and poets have reflected, with insight and acute observation, on them all.

My choice of poems to comment on is clearly personal, and another poetry lover could probably create a parallel collection of equal depth and merit, without including any overlapping texts, the pool of suitable poems is so huge. It has been painful to have to leave out so many possibilities, and the reader may be surprised by the absence of some obvious favourites. I have borne in mind the following principles: to include a wide range of types and stages of relationship; to find poems that, taken together, convey a lot of different things about love as well as demonstrating important common echoes; and not to repeat in this anthology any poems I have commented on in my other books (*The Heart's Time, Haphazard by Starlight* and *Our Last Awakening*).

In this anthology, the selected poems are grouped into sections: 'Up and down the generations'; 'Grown-up love'; 'God and the human heart'; and a short Postscript. The reader will find that there are many resonances between the sections, since we are constantly moved to understand one kind of love by reference to another: the earliest kind of love experienced by a needy infant is a startling image of God's love for us; an adult lover soothes his beloved to sleep almost as if he were singing a lullaby to a child; the restless searching of a passionate woman for her lost lover becomes a metaphor of the soul's seeking after God; and so on. In many of the poems, we see that images of the natural world are vital to conveying love's force and bodiliness: the changing seasons; the interplay of sunlight and darkness; outdoor activities like farming, mountain climbing, or walking in the woods or across the prairie; gazing at stars; following the flight of birds; watching the tides. It is as if we cannot love another without also being attentive to the vital details of the bodily world we live in. Love set us going; love formed us in the womb; we were made for love, and all our efforts at living well are nothing, if we lack love. And to love we shall return.

UP AND DOWN THE GENERATIONS

Human infants are born staggeringly vulnerable and help-less. Our brains are highly immature, our limbs lack any coordination, even our sight is unfocused. We are completely dependent on round-the-clock care, protection and feeding from an adult (who herself needs support to keep going with the care) for our very survival. Without the devoted attention of an adult, we will fail to thrive. And we need to receive at least 'good enough' love, which engages affectionately and calmly with us; otherwise our brains and bodies will not develop properly and we will not be able to enter human culture adequately or even manage our own moods. We need love in order to learn the language of human interaction and to become capable of expressing love ourselves. The experience of acute vulner-ability, and the experience of having that neediness responded to, is at the root of all that we know about love as adults.

The poems in this section deal with relationships between the generations. Many of them shift between the present moment and either the past or the future, acknowledging how this sort of love almost by definition is subject to change over time. Love of your children or your parents is constantly being reassessed over your lifetime. Parental love can be sentimentalized, but in reality it is both life-changing and utterly exhausting. It can be wonderful, but has its darker sides. Motherhood is something that comes as a shock to the system, as a woman comes to terms with the reality of a new life for which she is responsible ('Morning Song', p. 5). Parents can find themselves fantasizing that their child will fulfil dreams that have not happened in their lives ('Frost at Midnight', p. 9). Attentive motherhood can be so involved with a toddler that it becomes an almost predatory kind of love ('Child Waking', p. 13). It is quite possible to feel afraid of the furious demands of a baby ('Baby-Sitting', p. 17). A baby may be deeply beloved but also be a source of unending exhaustion, as it feels that your body, self, time and privacy have been completely taken over ('Our Lady of Vladimir', p. 21).

From the child's point of view, memories of one's mother may unlock a sense of helplessness ('Piano', p. 25). Love of a father may change from total hero worship in a small child to impatience with the elderly father as an adult ('Follower', p. 29). With the older generation, a grandfather may be a comforting figure to build one's identity on ('Climbing my Grandfather', p. 34); by contrast, a stern grandmother may represent a repressive religious faith which plants a sense of shame and anxiety within a pubertal granddaughter ('Staying at Grandma's' p. 38). An adult child who is left with the belongings of her deceased mother may come to realize for the first time something of the life and love her mother experienced before the child was born ('Handbag', p. 42).

Being the mother of more than one child is to witness whatever is the developing relationship between the siblings you have created. This is a potential love which is not under your control, but which may flourish and be proved after you are no longer there to see it ('The Rope', p. 46). Parenting is a kind of love that starts being wholly responsible for a child, but must gradually change and diminish in importance so that the child becomes capable of taking over as the grown-up – certainly in relation to their own offspring but perhaps even for the person who taught them to love, as she recedes into dementia ('What's in a name?' p. 51). The love that occurs between generations that care for one another is full of passion, ambiguity, change, and poignancy.

Morning Song

Love set you going like a fat gold watch.
The midwife slapped your footsoles, and your bald cry
Took its place among the elements.

Our voices echo, magnifying your arrival. New statue.
In a drafty museum, your nakedness
Shadows our safety. We stand round blankly as walls.

I'm no more your mother
Than the cloud that distills a mirror to reflect
        its own slow
Effacement at the wind's hand.

All night your moth-breath
Flickers among the flat pink roses. I wake to listen:
A far sea moves in my ear.

One cry, and I stumble from bed, cow-heavy and floral
In my Victorian nightgown.
Your mouth opens clean as a cat's. The window square

Whitens and swallows its dull stars. And now you try
Your handful of notes;
The clear vowels rise like balloons.

Sylvia Plath

'Love set you going.' The opening assertion of Plath's poem,
written after her daughter Frieda's birth in 1961, affirms the

obvious, fundamental necessity of love in creating and sustaining human life. Not only are we normally conceived in love, but we emerge, astonishingly helpless, into a world where we must be surrounded by persistent, reliable, long-term love in order to survive, develop our brains, grasp human culture and receive our very identity. It is no accident that the poem is addressed directly to the newborn child, like a love poem or 'aubade' (dawn serenade, morning song) to greet her birth, her first cry, her first night of life.

'Love set you going like a fat gold watch.' I think many poets would give their right arm to have written this line, it is so rich. At once philosophical and deeply comic, it makes reference to the Deist belief in a God who set the universe going like a divine watchmaker, who creates something very complex but then sits back and lets it tick on without further intervention. So the baby's birth is like a whole new creation. Yet the child is also 'like a fat gold watch': a small but solid item that used to be slipped out of a waistcoat pocket, and would fit snugly in the palm of the hand, still warm from the body of the wearer. Traditional gold watches were indeed fat, as they incorporated a chunky rounded lid that protected the watch face when tucked into a pocket. They were precious items, held close, and frequently gazed at. This yoking of the awesome and the everyday is completely appropriate to the experience of a mother who has just given birth.

Anyway, there is barely a moment to register this startlingly appropriate image before the child has been abruptly held upside down and slapped on her footsoles (this used to be the practice, to shock the baby into taking its first breath), and the child's 'bald cry' is heard. The word 'bald' is brilliant. Naturally, most babies are bald as they enter the world, with surreally large heads for their bodies. But the word also somehow conveys that distinctive, thin wail that characterizes the newborn cry; tender but completely unignorable, demanding its own 'place among the elements'. The child's voice announces the new reality that is the world now they are included in it.

But a birth does not herald only one new identity. It radically shifts all the previous relationships into a new phase as the parents are confronted with the reality of what is now asked of them. The next two stanzas reflect this sense of shock. It is as if the room where the birth has taken place has shifted into being a 'drafty museum' where a 'new statue' has suddenly arrived, at which the onlookers gaze in bemusement, not sure what to make of it. Motherhood can't be grasped or inhabited instantly; the narrator does not have a solid enough sense of her own identity. 'I'm no more your mother/ Than the cloud' – the image speaks of a 'slow effacement' as of a cloud dissolving in the wind (and this is a reasonable fear, given the actual demands of motherhood as they evolve).

Some commentators on 'Morning Song' express surprise that the poet only mentions the word 'love' right at the beginning, and consider that the poem is about a sense of alienation from the maternal love which should kick in straight away. But it seems to me that Plath exactly captures that insane attentiveness that characterizes new mothers, who cannot sleep for gazing at their newborn child, and straining to hear their every breath. She knows 'All night' how the child's 'moth-breath/ Flickers' – the image is precise and delicate. We sense the child's nearness, but also its elemental significance. Listening out for the baby, the mother hears 'A far sea' as well.

The penultimate stanza stumbles into action just as the new mother does, in response to 'One cry'. There is a lovely contrast between the moth-like child and the clumsy, post-partum mother yanked into responding instinctively to the child's demand. She is a comic blend of animal physicality and polite human culture, 'cow-heavy and floral/ In my Victorian nightgown'. But the child is so far just simple instinct: 'Your mouth opens clean as a cat's'.

The final stanza, though, seems to herald the baby's movement into intentional human self-expression, and it turns out that the 'morning song' of the title belongs to the baby, not the mother. The coming of dawn (which will be only too familiar to this breastfeeding mother over time) is conveyed in a downbeat way. There is nothing rosy-fingered about it; the window frame simply 'Whitens and swallows its dull stars'. Of course stars do appear more faint as daylight begins, but there is a sense that something is being erased. However, the child's voice, not now just a wail but a 'handful of notes' tried out for their sound, is celebrated like the rising of balloons, full of immediacy and joy.

Frost at Midnight

The Frost performs its secret ministry,
Unhelped by any wind. The owlet's cry
Came loud – and hark, again! loud as before.
The inmates of my cottage, all at rest,
Have left me to that solitude, which suits
Abstruser musings: save that at my side
My cradled infant slumbers peacefully . . .

Dear Babe, that sleepest cradled by my side,
Whose gentle breathings, heard in this deep calm,
Fill up the interspersèd vacancies
And momentary pauses of the thought!
My babe so beautiful! it thrills my heart
With tender gladness, thus to look at thee,
And think that thou shalt learn far other lore,
And in far other scenes! For I was reared
In the great city, pent 'mid cloisters dim,
And saw nought lovely but the sky and stars.
But *thou*, my babe! shalt wander like a breeze
By lakes and sandy shores, beneath the crags
Of ancient mountain, and beneath the clouds,
Which image in their bulk both lakes and shores
And mountain crags: so shalt thou see and hear
The lovely shapes and sounds intelligible
Of that eternal language, which thy God
Utters, who from eternity doth teach
Himself in all, and all things in himself.

Great universal Teacher! he shall mould
Thy spirit, and by giving make it ask.

Therefore all seasons shall be sweet to thee,
Whether the summer clothe the general earth
With greenness, or the redbreast sit and sing
Betwixt the tufts of snow on the bare branch
Of mossy apple tree, while the nigh thatch
Smokes in the sun-thaw; whether the eave-drops fall
Heard only in the trances of the blast,
Or if the secret ministry of frost
Shall hang them up in silent icicles,
Quietly shining to the quiet Moon.

Samuel Taylor Coleridge

Following Plath's famous poem of a new mother, this classic, delightful extract from a somewhat longer poem by Coleridge is chosen for the tenderness of tone of a new father, and his musings on his baby's hoped-for future.

The poem begins and ends with a sense of the 'secret ministry' of frost outside, while all the household apart from the narrator is asleep, including his infant son. We should imagine the speaker seated near the gradually sinking fire, in the living room, where the child's wooden rocking cradle also stands, this being the only part of the house that has been heated in the middle of winter. This is how it comes about that the father who has not yet gone to bed is alone with his sleeping baby.

The section omitted here includes the thoughts and memories that arise as the speaker gazes at the dying fire, and recalls his own boyhood – times when he has similarly watched the flames and let his imagination wander. There is an implication that his schoolroom was a deadening place for him, and that books and study have been poor teachers for the development of his soul. He contrasts his memories of constraints and boredom, 'pent 'mid cloisters dim', where he 'saw nought lovely but the sky and stars' with what he hopes will be his son's experience of learning. And these hopes are lyrical: 'But *thou*, my babe! shalt wander like a breeze/ By lakes and sandy shores, beneath the crags/ Of ancient mountain.' Coleridge, like his friend Wordsworth, was convinced of the power of the natural world to mould the growing soul of the child in ways that book learning could never do. He understands nature to be almost the 'book of God' himself. This philosophy is a strand of the Romantic movement which took hold as a counter-weight to the mechanism and hyper-rationality of Enlightenment thinking.

This vision may also owe something, as an educational strategy, to the idealism of Jean-Jacques Rousseau, who believed that children were 'noble savages' who would pretty much educate themselves if given complete freedom. But this free-ranging fantasy about what life could offer to one's own tiny child, who as yet is all potential (and has no identifiable limits or drawbacks), is a deeply recognizable kind of reverie. In a sense, new parents have only their own experience to draw on in formulating their hopes for their fiercely loved infant, and so there is a desire either to replicate for that child all that was most precious about their own childhood, or else to ensure that their problematic or tedious childhood experience is not repeated. Perhaps the child will be able to achieve his potential beyond that of his father.

And so 'Frost at Midnight', addressed to a sleeping infant, is undoubtedly much more about the narrator of the poem than about his son. The central image of the silent frost, beautiful as it is, may be conveying something about a paralysis in the poet's life, sleepless as he is. The last section of the poem has a poignant, bitter-sweet ring to it: 'Therefore all seasons shall be sweet to thee' is a beautiful blessing for a child – and yet is it not also a dearly held wish for the narrator himself? The range of possible seasons is not fully explored here. Summer greenness is briefly mentioned, but the image that is developed is that of a winter day that fluctuates between a brief period of thaw in the sunshine, and returning frost. The robin perches between 'tufts of snow'; the thatched roof 'Smokes in the sun-thaw'; but eventually the inevitable, freezing cold takes hold once more, transforming the dripping thatch eaves into 'silent icicles' again.

Child Waking

The child sleeps in the daytime,
With his abandoned, with his jetsam look,
On the bare mattress, across the cot's corner;
Covers and toys thrown out, a routine labour.

Relaxed in sleep and light,
Face upwards, never so clear a prey to eyes;
Like a walled town surprised out of the air –
All life called in, yet all laid bare

To the enemy above –
He has taken cover in daylight, gone to ground
In his own short length, his body strong in bleached
Blue cotton and his arms outstretched.

Now he opens eyes but not
To see at first; they reflect the light like snow,
And I wait in doubt if he sleeps or wakes, till I see
Slight pain of effort at the boundary

And hear how the trifling wound
Of bewilderment fetches a caverned cry
As he crosses out of sleep – at once to recover
His place and poise, and smile as I lift him over.

But I recall the blue-
White snowfield of his eyes empty of sight
High between dream and day, and think how there
The soul might rise visible as a flower.

E. J. Scovell

As we have seen, it is common for poets to reflect on their love for a baby or child while the latter are asleep. Initially, there is no other moment in which to stop and think. But it is also true that there is a compelling urge to gaze at a sleeping child; there is something about the space it allows for protective feelings to emerge – and the smooth, relaxed face of an infant is simply very beautiful.

This poem is interesting because it focuses on the child who is no longer a small baby, but may perhaps still be at the age that precedes speech (about 12 months?). This means that he is already implicitly conveying a distinct personality, but the adult who cares for him still needs to intuit his feelings, needs and reactions through attentive observation. He is also young enough to attract that hungry gaze of the mother who still cannot get enough of just looking at him with love. The child still sleeps in a cot, and he has been put down, fully dressed, for the daytime nap which all toddlers require until they are old enough to make it through a whole day. The speaker is watching him just before and just as he 'comes to' into a world of daylight, and the poem seeks to capture the essence of the child, 'the soul' at the moment between sleep and waking.

The picture of the boy in his daytime sleep will be deeply recognizable to anyone who has supervised a toddler. In his floating relaxation, he is almost like driftwood on the waves, 'with his jetsam look'. Before entering this 'abandoned' state of sleep, he has systematically jettisoned from the cot everything the adult provided for his rest. This is his regular habit: 'Covers and toys thrown out, a routine labour.' He has ended up in a strange position 'across the cot's corner', as if suddenly arrested by sleep, rather than having comfortably composed himself to allow sleep to come.

The second and third stanzas address how exposed this leaves the child to being lovingly inspected by his mother, yet a strangely sinister, almost predatory tone emerges. His face and body are 'never so clear a prey to eyes', so the mother's gaze seems not wholly innocent: the loving gaze may have a certain 'devouring' element to it. The next image only intensifies this suggestion: the upright bars of the cot, with the adult leaning over them, suggest 'a walled town surprised out of the air'. The word 'enemy' is actually used, as if the boy is right to try and escape the adult's desire to hunt down and grasp his essence. Interestingly, the extended metaphor is concluded in a way that grants the child a capacity to be his own person, unaffected by what his supervising adult is wanting to know. Though the language speaks of defensive action against surveillance ('He has taken cover', 'gone to ground'), it is as if his selfhood is firmly contained within his own small body, which is 'strong in bleached/ Blue cotton'. Toddlers can be surprisingly strong, with firm little bodies and robust, full-sized, determined egos.

The second half of the poem describes, in beautifully observed detail, the actual moment when the toddler wakes up and realizes where he is. Our attention is drawn to his eyes, which momentarily are still focused on an internal dream, and not yet on his surroundings. This leaves them in a way strangely vacant, reflecting light 'like snow' (and perhaps, it is implied, transforming the territory of his gaze rather as snow does in the landscape). The poet notices the child's 'Slight pain of effort at the boundary', his 'trifling wound/ Of bewilderment' as he moves into ordinary consciousness. These brief and minuscule moments of distress bring forth first an elemental 'caverned cry', and then, very swiftly, a 'smile as I lift him over'. As all of us do at this moment of awakening, the child recovers his 'place and poise' as a social being greeting someone he loves.

But it is this key moment, which shifts away almost as soon as it happens, which seems to the poet to reveal the child's soul, who he really is. This is what the speaker of the poem responds to in love, even if the language and imagery of the text suggest that there is something invasive about wanting to apprehend such an intimate aspect of another person.

Baby-Sitting

I am sitting in a strange room listening
For the wrong baby. I don't love
This baby. She is sleeping a snuffly
Roseate, bubbling sleep; she is fair;
She is a perfectly acceptable child.
I am afraid of her. If she wakes
She will hate me. She will shout
Her hot midnight rage, her nose
Will stream disgustingly and the perfume
Of her breath will fail to enchant me.

To her I will represent absolute
Abandonment. For her it will be worse
Than for the lover cold in lonely
Sheets; worse than for the woman who waits
A moment to collect her dignity
Beside the bleached bone in the terminal ward.
As she rises sobbing from the monstrous land
Stretching for milk-familiar comforting,
She will find me and between us two
It will not come. It will not come.

Gillian Clarke

In this poem, Gillian Clarke explores the powerful nature of the love we feel for our infants, by examining, in a rather uncomfortable way, what it is like when an adult is responsible for a baby that they *don't* love. The speaker in the poem is a baby-sitter; so she is bound to be at least a trusted friend of the baby's parents, and she has obviously agreed to take on this responsibility.

But she discovers that she cannot inhabit the role she has taken on: it feels all wrong; she is out of place; nothing 'fits' between her and her charge: 'I am sitting in a strange room listening/ For the wrong baby.' The implication is that she already has experience of listening out for the 'right' baby, namely a child of her own, and this is how she grasps what is out of kilter in her situation: 'I don't love/ This baby.' The bald statement is shocking, because an impulse to protect tiny infants is supposed to be hard-wired into human beings. And it may be, but what is highlighted here is the overriding importance of love, especially perhaps that visceral sort of love that is the bond between the breastfeeding mother and the child she suckles.

The series of statements about the baby that follow this stark admission about a lack of love gradually explain what the baby-sitter means, and draw the reader on to experience something of what she is feeling. Initially the comments about the child are completely positive, though quite detailed about the quality of her sleep: 'She is sleeping a snuffly/ Roseate, bubbling sleep; she is fair.' The word 'roseate' is a lovely, precise description of the baby's face, and has a kind of charm that is also reflected in the words 'snuffly' and 'bubbling', with their mutual assonance. However, it is gradually becoming clear that the child has a cold. The next sentence, 'She is a perfectly acceptable child', has several sorts of impact. At one level it is clearly just the case. At another, this is not what people say about sweet little babies when they feel warmly towards them. At the very least, it contains a huge implicit 'but' within the statement.

And the next sentence makes clear what the misgiving is: 'I am afraid of her. If she wakes/ She will hate me.' The baby-sitter is afraid, because a child with a streaming nose is very likely to have broken sleep, and could therefore wake up, distressed, at any moment. It is interesting the power that an infant has over an adult who knows she will be unable to comfort the child or give her what she wants and needs. The adult who feels no visceral love is afraid of the child who demands it, because the adult's helplessness will thus be revealed. This adult certainly knows what comes next. The absolute, uncompromising rage of the infant, and the consequential disgusting torrent of snot, will transform a perfectly acceptable child into a raging monster, the perfume of whose breath 'will fail to enchant me'. By this stage, the reader is probably sharing the disgust foreseen by the baby-sitter.

But then the poem turns, as she realizes that the failure lies in herself, not in the child. The second stanza embraces the perspective of the baby who has been abandoned to the 'wrong' person, who may be technically responsible but is not familiar and cannot in fact offer 'milk-familiar comforting'. It is not the baby who doesn't smell right, but the adult, who isn't lactating. The absence of love is devastating, and final: 'She will find me and between us two/ It will not come. It will not come.' The poet compares the baby's grief to the massive losses experienced by adults: the deserted lover 'cold in lonely/ Sheets'; the bereaved wife who has been watching at the deathbed of her beloved. These comparisons instantly give a dignity to the anticipated, immediate rage of the sleeping child, and of course they remind us of losses to come.

The poem is a fascinating investigation of how important the visceral, bodily connection is with a tiny baby, and how that isn't always present in those who care for a child. But through its mention of future griefs, I think it touches on an anxiety which is central to parental love also. This is the awareness that, while a breastfeeding mother may indeed temporarily be all in all to a child, this stage doesn't last, and none of us can protect our children, even with all the love we have for them, from the inevitable pains and losses that love will bring in its wake during their lifetime. This includes the pain of love that is wanted but is not reciprocated, or that cannot be generated at will just because it is needed or desired.

Our Lady of Vladimir

Climbs the child, confident,
up over breast, arm, shoulder;
while she, alarmed by his bold thrust
into her face, and the encircling hand,
looks out imploring fearfully
and, O, she cries, from her immeasurable eyes,
O how he clings, see how
he smothers every pore, like the soft
shining mistletoe to my black bark,
she says, I cannot breathe, my eyes
are aching so.

The child has overlaid us in our beds,
we cannot close our eyes,
his weight sits firmly,
fits over heart and lungs,
and choked we turn away
into the window of immeasurable dark
to shake off the insistent pushing warmth;
O how he cleaves, no peace
tonight my lady in your bower,
you, like us, restless with bruised eyes
and waking to

a shining cry on the black bark of sleep.

Rowan Williams

This remarkable poem is based on one of the most famous religious pictures of the Virgin and Child, the twelfth-century Byzantine icon called Our Lady of Vladimir. It is of very fine quality, and has been copied many times. As the mother of Jesus, Mary is known as *theotokos* or 'birth-giver of God'. The background is of beaten gold, the child wears a gown of gold thread, and Mary wears a black veil edged with gold braiding, the darkness of her clothes matching that of her eyes, which gaze out at the viewer. The child's eyes are fixed on his mother, and he is energetically snuggling up, pushing his cheek against Mary's, and wrapping his arm around her neck. It is an icon that is called an icon of tenderness, or loving-kindness.

But it is somewhat disturbing rather than comforting or sentimental, and the poet here captures the unsettling nature of the image. The poem starts right in with the child's action in pressing against his mother, one might almost say invading her space: 'Climbs the child, confident,/ up over breast, arm, shoulder'. The alliterated hard 'c's emphasize the child's insistence. As a religious image it is surprising, but of course this is exactly what real babies do, as soon as they develop the strength to stand up firmly in their mother's lap, and grab her chin, hair or clothes. The needy and determined love of a small child who still needs to be carried demands total attention and recognizes no personal boundaries. This is why parents look so exhausted and even burdened during the first year of a child's life, even as they experience adoration for a person who has turned their lives upside down. It is at one level delightful to care for a baby who loves to fit so snugly and perpetually to your body. It is also completely understandable that you sometimes feel you want your body back.

So this Mary, rather than presenting simply a holy serenity, appears to be longing for a break from her burden of love, he clings so closely. She has the hollow-eyed look of many an insomniac parent. The poet even has her describe the child as like a parasite – as if he is 'shining mistletoe to my black bark'. And yet this is an image of the Christ child, an image of the incarnate God. Rowan Williams has written elsewhere about this icon, in his book *Ponder These Things*, explaining how an ordinary child's invasive, eager love is an appropriate reflection of God's love for us. God's love here

> is that of an eager and rather boisterous child, scrambling up on his mother's lap, seizing handfuls of her clothing and nuzzling his face against hers, with that extraordinary hunger for sheer physical closeness that children will show with loving parents . . . This is a child who cannot bear to be separated from his mother.[1]

As an image of God, it is bold and shameless, and Williams points out that dealing with the burden of such love might well leave Mary looking overwhelmed and fearful. For as Williams remarks, 'To be the object of any intense and passionate human love when we do not know how to respond, or do not know *whether* we can respond, is always pretty frightening and sobering.'[2]

For the second stanza takes the image of invasion even further: 'The child has overlaid us in our beds.' This is a reversal of the age-old fear that parents have that they might accidentally overlay and smother their child during sleep; here it is we, the parents, who fear for our capacity to breathe, we feel so smothered and choked by his attention. Though the poet is drawing on what seem like the endless sleepless nights of new parents, I think the problem here has firmly become the Christ child. It is God himself whose 'insistent pushing warmth' we attempt to shake off, only to discover that the alternative is a 'window of immeasurable dark' (the same word that described Mary's pained eyes in the first stanza).

And so we are presented with a surprising and not wholly comfortable image of what it might be like to be loved by God and not to be able to resist. It is very like having a baby, without having a clue what demands that person will make on your love, your resilience, your boundaries, your energy, and the pattern of your days for ever after. As Williams puts it, just like a baby, 'God wills not to be separated from us, not to be shut out from any corner of our being.'[3]

Piano

Softly, in the dusk, a woman is singing to me
Taking me back down the vista of years, till I see
A child sitting under the piano, in the boom of the
       tingling strings
And pressing the small, poised feet of a mother who
       smiles as she sings.

In spite of myself, the insidious mastery of song
Betrays me back, till the heart of me weeps to belong
To the old Sunday evenings at home, with winter
       outside
And hymns in the cosy parlour, the tinkling piano
       our guide.

So now it is vain for the singer to burst into clamour
With the great black piano appassionato. The glamour
Of childish days is upon me, my manhood is cast
Down in a flood of remembrance, I weep like a child
       for the past.

D. H. Lawrence

The focus of this poem is not a child whom the narrator is
gazing at – as a person or an icon – but the speaker's own self
as a child, in relation to his mother. The occasion is vaguely
sketched; whether the speaker is listening to someone who
is performing just for him or is part of a gathering (perhaps
in a drawing room which has a grand piano), he feels that 'a

woman is singing to me'. It was still the case in the early part of the twentieth century that women were expected to develop certain accomplishments, including proficiency in playing the piano and singing for the after-dinner entertainment of the company, especially the men. While some men did also perform, there was a gendered expectation here, and the poem seems to capture the importance of being a man who is sung to by a woman, and the surprisingly deep emotions potentially connected with this well-bred tradition.

After establishing the scene, the poem immediately travels 'back down the vista of years', and we find ourselves in the startling position of being a small person sitting underneath a piano while it is being played. I can bear witness from my own childhood that this is a very interesting and compelling place to sit. An upright piano used to be a feature of every home that aspired to any sort of musical culture – and this was not only middle-class households, in the days when making music yourself was the only way to experience it at home. And, in contrast with a digital keyboard, the piano mechanism involves internal strings being hammered and made to vibrate as the keys are pressed. So, if you sat beneath an upright piano, your back rested against a panel that covered these vibrating strings, and you felt the music go right through your body. You did get a slightly distorted sense of the sound, so the 'boom of the tingling strings' is rather precisely put. At the same time, you were sitting right where the piano player is using her feet to press the loud and soft pedals, and you could have fun pressing those feet to join in with the performance. Here we have a sense of the appearance and character of the speaker's mother, through what her feet are like – 'small' and 'poised'. Clearly a feminine woman, you have the sense that she was indulgent to the child rather than annoyed by him. He asserts that she 'smiles as she sings'. This is something he could not have observed from his position beneath the piano, but perhaps he could hear it in her voice.

The second verse speaks of how the 'insidious mastery' of song (this is an interesting word to use, seeing that in this case it is exercised by women, both now and in the past) takes him back to memories of Sunday evening hymn-singing round the piano. The narrator uses the word 'betrays', as if this experience of being taken out of himself and back to his child-hood is somehow an undermining one. Certainly present-day understanding of music's capacity to generate powerful and often poignant memories from way back is widely used in contexts such as care homes for the elderly, including those with dementia. But the effect is normally comforting. Perhaps it depends how willing one is to identify with one's much younger self, even when the memories are benign. Here it seems that the memory is of cosiness, togetherness and happy music-making. But perhaps there is a sense of faith that has lapsed somewhat, of hymns that are no longer straightforward for the adult man?

The third verse begins by returning to the music that is being made in the present moment in which the poem is set, and the performer seems to be reaching a crescendo in her music. The 'great black piano' is being played 'appassionato' (passionately). Perhaps the suggestion is of powerful and quite erotic, adult feeling behind the playing. But creating a telling rhyme between the immediate 'clamour' of the con-temporary performance and the 'glamour' of the childhood memory, the poem gives the greater power to the memory. 'Glamour' has the archaic resonances of a magic spell, not wholly comfortable, rather than the modern sense which we associate with a confident and deeply attractive woman. The seductive situation of the present collapses before the flood of childhood remembrance, and this is why the narrator asserts that 'my manhood is cast/ Down' by it. He may only mean his manhood in the sense of his capacity to resist bursting into tears; but you have the sense that his petite, musical mother who played and sang to him as a child is for him the template for all womanhood thereafter. And no one will measure up to her.

Follower

My father worked with a horse-plough,
His shoulders globed like a full sail strung
Between the shafts and the furrow.
The horses strained at his clicking tongue.

An expert. He would set the wing
And fit the bright steel-pointed sock.
The sod rolled over without breaking.
At the headrig, with a single-pluck

Of reins, the sweating team turned round
And back into the land. His eye
Narrowed and angled at the ground,
Mapping the furrow exactly.

I stumbled in his hobnailed wake,
Fell sometimes on the polished sod;
Sometimes he rode me on his back
Dipping and rising to his plod.

I wanted to grow up and plough,
To close one eye, stiffen my arm.
All I ever did was follow
In his broad shadow round the farm.

I was a nuisance, tripping, falling,
Yapping always. But today
It is my father who keeps stumbling
Behind me, and will not go away.

Seamus Heaney

This poem starts with the perspective of the child, in this case contemplating his father. From the start it is clear that the narrator is looking back through the eyes of his remembered childhood on a farm, and for five full verses we have a beautifully realized, detailed memory of watching his beloved father, as a competent and strong young man, ploughing his fields. He remembers how he used to try and keep up, following a father who gently included him. Only in the very last verse does the poem draw back and consider how irritating he must have been to deal with, in the middle of this difficult work. And then there is a second, terrible shift in perspective as the poem ends, as it switches from the examination of a child's hero-worshipping love for his father, to an almost complete reversal in the adult narrator now.

The poem's title, 'Follower', places us exactly in the position which the small child necessarily adopted in the past when observing the process of ploughing close up, and it conveys both practical accuracy and a sense of adoring discipleship. This is an observer who wants to be close to his heroic father, to see exactly how the work is done, and longs to grow up and be strong enough to do that work for himself. Of course, the fact that we are reading a literary work by someone famous, who clearly did not end up running a farm for a living, adds a sense of poignancy to the narrative and lets us know that this dream did not survive. In any case, we are immediately made aware that his father's work belongs in a bygone era, since he 'worked with a horse-plough' – technology which was soon superseded. The poem is like a luminous but sepia photograph of the past, which, like childhood, is no longer accessible to the adult man.

The form of the poem is quite controlled, with regular four-line stanzas, where the first and third line endings have half-rhymes, and the second and fourth usually have full rhymes, placing a firm emphasis on the conclusion of each verse. This regularity mirrors the absolute concentration and control that needed to be exercised by the ploughman in order to achieve the difficult work of precision ploughing with a team of heavy horses and traditional, hand-held tools.

What the small child remembers most clearly is his father's back view, and the way his muscles are engaged in the work. The focus is on his shoulders and the bunch of the muscles are 'globed like a full sail'. The visual image of a full sail suggests smooth, tense power, and a form of transport where there is no mechanical assistance, only wind-power. The man must be 'strung/ Between the shafts and the furrow', directing the accuracy of the operation by controlling the mighty horse-power by nothing more than 'his clicking tongue'. For those of us who do not remember a time before mechanization, it is instructive to appreciate the sheer physical skill and strength that used to be necessary.

The next two stanzas describe exactly what it took to become 'An expert'. The business end of the ploughshare, its 'bright steel-pointed sock' that cuts the furrow, had to be fitted right. The wing held the direction steady, and the controlled speed of the horses who pulled the plough meant that 'The sod rolled over without breaking'.

Then, at the end of the field, the whole team needed to be turned to smoothly start the return furrow. The poem conveys how skilfully this was done by having the effective 'single-pluck/ Of reins' sit across the turn from one stanza to the next. This breaks the usual end-stop of the verse but continues the movement of the sense onwards like the unceasing plough. Then it emphasizes the importance of the man's focused eye, constantly making judgements about distance and speed, in holding the activity together.

Next, we turn to look at the little child and his experience amid this steely focus. We are down at the level of the hob-nailed boots and the difficulty of negotiating the stiff turns of the ploughed earth, which looks almost 'polished', so crisply has the ploughshare cut the sod. The stumbling child is lifted up to the ploughman's shoulders so he could ride – the 'Dipping and rising' makes him part of the whole rhythm of the work (though surely this was quite a burden for the man). And we hear of his passionate longing to be able to 'grow up and plough', using his eyes and his arms in the same efficient way. Then the narrator distances himself through his knowledge of what actually transpired, and there is disappointment about what he did not grow up to do: 'All I ever did was follow/ In his broad shadow'.

He passes judgement on his childish self: 'I was a nuisance, tripping, falling,/ Yapping always.' It is not clear that his father ever regarded him as a nuisance, but the narrator sees his own physical deficits; and his own facility with words is described in derogatory terms, 'Yapping'. But then he charts his own realization of how he passes judgement on his father, who has now become old and frail, while his son is grown up. For the one-time ploughman now stumbles with old age and tries hopelessly to keep up with his son, and what that son has become. Does the son gently seek to include him? No, he just notices that he 'will not go away'.

Climbing my Grandfather

I decide to do it free, without a rope or net.
First, the old brogues, dusty and cracked;
an easy scramble onto his trousers,
pushing into the weave, trying to get a grip.
By the overhanging shirt I change
direction, traverse along his belt
to an earth stained hand. The nails
are splintered and give good purchase,
the skin of his finger is smooth and thick
like warm ice. On his arm I discover
the glassy ridge of a scar, place my feet
gently in the old stitches and move on.
At his still firm shoulder, I rest for a while
in the shade, not looking down,
for climbing has its dangers, then pull
myself up the loose skin of his neck
to a smiling mouth to drink among teeth.
Refreshed, I cross the screed cheek,
to stare into his brown eyes, watch a pupil
slowly open and close. Then up over
the forehead, the wrinkles well-spaced
and easy, to his thick hair (soft and white
at this altitude), reaching for the summit,
where gasping for breath I can only lie
watching clouds and birds circle,
feeling his heat, knowing
the slow pulse of his good heart.

Andrew Waterhouse

When it comes to relationships across two generations, the dynamic of love may be different. A growing child may feel less ambivalent towards a grandparent as he or she becomes increasingly independent, as there is not the same need, as with a parent, to find ways to break free and establish one's own distinct identity. A grandparent can remain as a consistent, rock-solid support and comfort, providing something to build on, or, as in this poem, something to climb on.

The title establishes this process immediately, and the reader at first envisages a very young child, who is small enough to climb up an accommodating adult's body, and find that a triumphant achievement. Yet the way the poem talks about the enterprise presupposes an adult speaker, who is a confident rock climber, capable of tackling a challenging climb 'free, without a rope or net'. And this metaphor of the grandfather's body as a tricky but satisfying climb pervades the whole poem, creating some amusing analogies while establishing the grandfather as a loving bodily presence who roots his grandson's sense of self as he gradually adds to his achievements in this world.

In order to pursue the dominant metaphor, we begin to see the climber and the 'cliff' as occupying contrasting sizes in space. Either the speaker is like a Lilliputian figure (and Gulliver's travels do come to mind), or the speaker is life-size but the grandfather is a benign giant who allows this tiny little man to scramble right up to the summit of his head. As the climb proceeds, we get a graphic picture of the old man and what he is wearing, with the signs of age and old, healed wounds, and how his body and face convey his warm, resilient character. The poem is in a single paragraph, without breaks or stanzas, and this form mirrors a continuous climb right to the top without a significant pause.

At every stage, starting from the dusty 'old brogues', the poem holds together the texture of the man's body along with the mountaineering challenge. The terms belong in the world of climbing: 'easy scramble', 'trying to get a grip', 'traverse', 'good purchase', but are comically related to the grandfather's clothes and body. He has an 'overhanging shirt' – both a tough part of the climb and an indication that either he is a bit scruffy and doesn't tuck his shirt in, or there is a significant overhang of belly over his belt, which requires a sideways movement to negotiate. Arriving at the earth-stained hand with splintered nails, the narrator seems to focus on what kind of terrain this presents to the climber, but of course it also implies what sort of life and occupation the man has had. He has worked with his hands, and there is something very comforting and 'earthing' about what physical labour has done to them. The details of hands are something a small child notices and draws attention to, without judgement.

When the climber reaches the arm (the sleeves seem to be rolled up), it is as if he makes a discovery that is useful to climb with, namely 'the glassy ridge of a scar' which he can use for footholds as he continues on up. But he is also noticing that his grandfather bears the marks of an old wound which required stitches – perhaps an industrial injury of some kind. Wounds, and the resilience to heal and 'move on', may have something important to teach about dealing with life and what it hits us with. At the top of the arm, where the shoulder is 'still firm' (safe ground to stop at, testimony to continuing strength in older age), the climber rests, but without looking down, as 'climbing has its dangers'.

The next part manages to mingle the signs of advanced age, which we might normally see as regrettable (loose skin round the neck, a certain amount of drooling between the teeth, strongly established wrinkles, white hair), and landscape that is enabling or exciting for a climber (something to pull yourself up on; a place to drink and be refreshed; easy, well-spaced footholds, and the exhilaration of a snowy summit). The whole poem conveys beautifully the small child's non-judgemental curiosity and delight in the aged body of a grandparent, and the feelings of safety it can convey. At the same time, the child's love just takes all this for granted and instinctively makes it part of his growing up, adopting challenges, facing dangers and celebrating his own achievements.

Staying at Grandma's

Sometimes they left me for the day
while they went – what does it matter
where – away. I sat and watched her work
the dough, then turn the white shape
yellow in a buttered bowl.

A coleus, wrong to my eye because its leaves
were red, was rooting on the sill
in a glass filled with water and azure
marbles. I loved to see the sun
pass through the blue.

'You know,' she'd say, turning
her straight and handsome back to me,
'that the body is the temple
of the Holy Ghost.'

The Holy Ghost, the oh, oh . . . the *uh*
oh, I thought, studying the toe of my new shoe,
and glad she wasn't looking at me.

Soon I'd be back in school. No more mornings
at Grandma's side while she swept the walk
or shook the dust mop by the neck.

If she loved me why did she say that
two women would be grinding at the mill,
that God would come out of the clouds

when they were least expecting him,
choose one to be with him in heaven
and leave the other there alone?

Jane Kenyon

This is a very different memory of a grandparent from that of the previous poem. Grandma, so far from engendering a sense of safety, or a place from which the delighted grand-daughter could launch her own adventures, actually strikes a chill into the child's soul.

This poem leaves a great deal implied rather than spelt out. Key visual details are there, but there is no real sense of a warm relationship; indeed, we do not see Grandma's face at all, only her 'straight and handsome back'. There is engagement between the generations here, but it is of a very uncomfortable kind. All that this upright back communicates is a fearsome set of religious standards, as it seems that Grandma has decided to begin a conversation that the child would very much rather not have, and in which neither of them want to look at the other's face. You have the sense that the child is perhaps just on the cusp of puberty: young enough to need a caretaker but old enough (just) for the subject of sexual behaviour to be broached, albeit in an elliptical fashion.

Grandma's home is clearly not one that the child warmed to, or would have chosen to stay if she had not been obliged to. Her memory is that her parents (just referred to as 'they') left her there without negotiation because of other places they had to be. The child has forgotten, or had no context for under-standing why she has been dumped at Grandma's. They just went away, 'what does it matter/ where'. Grandma herself does not cease from continuing with her housework to attend to the child, but instead relates to her without looking at her directly. Gazing around, the child notes that the house itself has rather vivid, beautiful features. She recalls seeing the way the pastry dough turns yellower in the bowl as butter is added; she remembers the red coleus leaves, and the intense azure blue of the marbles in the rooting water on the window sill. There is a child's attention to the distinctive features of the grandparental home or kitchen routine, and there is warmth in the memory of the sunlight through glass. Yet even here there is a sense of unease. The coleus was 'wrong to my eye because its leaves/ were red'. A non-green plant is somehow disturbing.

Grandma speaks for the first time, and her 'You know', as she actually turns her back, is not reassuring. It is as if she has gone straight into the ensuing sermon without preamble: 'the body is the temple/ of the Holy Ghost.' Now any girl of my generation who grew up in an evangelical religious household was bound to get this instruction sooner or later. I have no idea whether boys got told this as well; I suspect not, even though St Paul was largely addressing men in 1 Corinthians 6.12–19. In Corinth, Paul's teaching about the gospel super-seding the constraints of the Jewish law had been freely interpreted by some to mean that 'anything goes', including in sexual behaviour. So Paul is engaged in rowing back and pointing out that, while all things are lawful, not everything is helpful, and he concludes the argument with the image of a holy temple, which must be preserved as pure.

The poem shows the child taking a moment or two to get what on earth Grandma is on about; this is graphically depicted by a series of grunts: 'The Holy Ghost, the oh, oh . . . the *uh/ oh*, I thought.' Squirming embarrassment is expressed by 'studying the toe of my new shoe' – perhaps wishing she had a Grandma who, instead of embarking on alarming scriptural injunctions, would just be delighted by a recent retail purchase that gave her granddaughter pleasure. The new shoe possibly implies the end of summer approaching, and the prospect of school paradoxically suggests freedom for the child, from a chilly relative whose unceasing 'cleanliness next to godliness' housework is described in punitive terms, as she 'shook the dust mop by the neck'.

The final paragraph addresses the question of love. At one level it is simply musing about the way she failed to experience as loving a Grandma who communicated only in alarming religious language. For here is another familiar trope of fundamentalist faith, namely a dwelling on the prospect of imminent apocalypse as a means of warning people to stay faithful. This refers to the passage in Luke 17.22–37, where Jesus predicts the sufferings of the end-time. Many images and earlier references are used, including Noah's flood, the destruction of Sodom, and the dreadful fate of Lot's wife. But the image this poem grasps is the fearful one of the two women using a two-handed millstone and grinding corn together, where one is 'taken' and the other left. The desolation of being left there alone mirrors the gloomy resignation of the poem's opening, where 'they left me for the day'.

The poem's question about Grandma is a very fair one: 'If she loved me why did she say that?' But the underlying question is also about God. If God loves us why are two women to be divided for ever – in Scripture or in the world of this poem?

Handbag

My mother's old leather handbag,
crowded with letters she carried
all through the war. The smell
of my mother's handbag: mints
and lipstick and Coty powder.
The look of those letters, softened
and worn at the edges, opened,
read, and refolded so often.
Letters from my father. Odour
of leather and powder, which ever
since then has meant womanliness,
and love, and anguish, and war.

Ruth Fainlight

As a child grows into an adult herself, and eventually reaches an age where her parents have died, there is a period of review about what those relationships have meant and how they have shaped her life. A particular feature of later life is the inheritance of the personal objects belonging to the older generation – some of them perhaps very private, but very revealing of the inner life of the one to whom they belonged. The grown-up, probably middle-aged child finds herself handling, and needing to deal with, items like a mother's handbag. It is in the nature of the relationship between a child and her mother that the mother's own individual identity, with its passions, anxieties and interests, is not really observed by the child while her primary role is that of the child's mother.

It can be a surprise and even a shock to realize that one's deceased parents had worries and love lives just as we do.

This poem focuses on the narrator's dead mother's handbag. The poem is brief and economical – handbag-sized, if you like. It operates without a single transitive verb, so you have the sense that the poet is just recording immediate impressions as she touches and opens the bag and reacts to its contents, without drawing any firm conclusions. And yet it also feels as if this is something she has contemplated and handled many times, perhaps, because of its significance, unable to throw it away.

The handbag and its contents are conveyed through powerful sense impressions, along with what the narrator knows about how these objects were treated by its owner: 'My mother's old leather handbag,/ crowded with letters she carried/ all through the war.' We never learn the details of what was contained in the letters; we do not need to. It is even possible that the narrator herself has never actually read what is in these letters. That might be a step too far in accessing the intimacy that was between her own parents. It is sufficient to know that the bag was 'crowded' with letters that were carried everywhere the handbag's owner went, for six whole years. 'Crowded' is a brilliant adjective. Many contemporary handbags are messy and over-full. This one contained a whole community of love messages, summing up the importance of a relationship that could not be pursued and enjoyed in the flesh for an intolerable length of time. At a time when phoning was impossible, texts or emails did not exist, and letters themselves were censored and could take weeks to arrive, these pieces of paper were beyond precious, as physical embodiments of love at a distance.

The next observation is about the distinctive smell of the inside of the handbag: 'mints/ and lipstick and Coty powder'. This combination is spot on for anyone of the generation whose mother went through the war; this is what women carried in their stiff, rather smart bags. Smell is well recognized as a sense that can recall memories in an instantaneous way, giving access to childhood experiences that cannot quite be remembered visually. The handbag was of magnetic interest, but with a forbidden scent.

Then the 'look of those letters' is highlighted. It is the sheer physicality of the letters which counts, 'softened/ and worn at the edges' from all the re-reading, re-folding, and from being carried endlessly in a handbag. We are asked to see what has been done with these bits of paper, rather than what is written on them. Although this has been implied throughout, the poem finally explains who they are from: 'Letters from my father.' It is interesting that the writer is identified by his relationship to the child. But what this establishes is that, although it is her mother's behaviour towards them that she is describing, their almost sacred quality involves what they stand for not just to the woman but to the child.

Again, 'odour' is mentioned, this time that distinctive combination of leather and powder which emanated from the handbag, and the poem suddenly enlarges the meaning of this inheritance. The odour is not just about her childhood memory, but about the speaker's whole adult identity, and her grasp of how people live their lives and experience the suffering and joys of love, caught up as they may be in much larger political realities of their time. That particular odour 'ever/ since then has meant womanliness,/ and love, and anguish, and war'.

The Rope

I have paused in the door jamb's shadow to watch you
    playing Shop or Cliff! or Café or Under-the-Sea
among the flotsam of props on our tarmacked
    driveway.
    All courtship. All courtesy.

At eight and six, you have discovered yourselves
    friends,
    at last, and this the surprise the summer
has gifted me, as if some
    penny-cum-handkerchief conjuror

had let loose a kingfisher . . .
    You whirl and pirouette, as in a ballet,
take decorous turns, and pay for whatever you need
    with a witch's currency:

grass cuttings, sea glass, coal, an archaeopteryx
    of glued kindling from the fire basket;
you don two invisible outsize overcoats – for love?
    for luck? – and jump with your eyes shut.

And I can almost see it thicken between you,
    your sibling-tetheredness, an umbilicus,
fattened on mornings like this as on a mother's blood,
    loose, translucent, not yet in focus,

but incipient as yeast and already strong enough
     to knock both of you off your balance
when you least expect it, some afternoon after work,
     decades hence,

one call from a far-flung city and, look,
     all variegated possibles – lovers, kids,
          apartments –
whiten into mist; the rope is flexing,
     tugging you close and you come, obedient

children that you are, back to this moment,
     staggering to a halt and then straightening,
grown little again inside your oversize coats and shoes
     and with sea glass still to arrange, but without me
          watching.

Sinéad Morrissey

This carefully observed and reflective poem shows a mother
of two small girls stepping back to ponder the nature of sis-
terhood, or 'sibling-tetheredness' as she puts it. She is shown
minding her daughters one summer morning, and, because
they are both old enough to play quite complex and involved
games of make-believe together (a new development, the
mother realizes), she has the space to look ahead to a time
when they are grown-up sisters – will this kind of connection
('The Rope') still exist? It is a meditation on a kind of love

that parents cannot of themselves create or force, namely the love that may subsist between siblings – or may not.

The poem is fairly regular, in stanzas with four lines each. They are often rather long lines, as if the narrator is letting her thoughts meander, just as her eye wanders lovingly over the charming details of the girls' play. The lines do not exactly rhyme, or match each other for rhythm, but there is a certain sense of form, with each second and fourth line in each stanza holding a half-rhyme (umbilicus/focus; balance/hence; apartments/obedient, and so on). This just suggests an echo without thumping to any conclusions, just as the poem itself is speculative rather than certain about how the relationship may develop.

The meditation starts slowly, as the narrator has 'paused in the door jamb's shadow to watch you'. This very convoluted way of describing the exact place the mother has taken up, in order to observe the girls discreetly, makes readers of the poem also slow down as they approach (it is hard to say this line quickly, if you read it out loud). The games her daughters are playing are not fully explained, perhaps because the inwardness of the games is accessible only to these two little girls. They are just given their titles: 'Shop or Cliff! or Café or Under-the-Sea'. This is sufficient code, and any pair of small siblings will have their own equivalents. There is a lovely contrast between the random nature of what is available for play ('the flotsam of props') and the highly rule-bound nature of the play itself ('All courtship. All courtesy').

The poem takes four stanzas to set out what has been happening this summer, which for the mother is a magical and totally surprising gift. Clearly accustomed to dealing with daughters who have quite different needs, or who are rivals for her attention rather than playmates, or who may have been displaying mutual hostility, suddenly she is free to watch a level of engaged play which does not in fact involve her any more. The freedom and artistry between the children are a delight; she uses images of a ballet, and observes a kind of decorum about taking turns which she has no doubt been striving to instil for years. The details of the chance items that can be commandeered for play are lively and sometimes startling. The 'witch's currency' the girls pay each other in includes 'grass cuttings, sea glass, an archaeopteryx/ of glued kindling from the fire basket'. Dinosaurs can lurk in everyday items.

Exactly halfway through the poem there is a sort of turn, as the narrator steps back from the scene she is describing and with it conjures the vision of a new kind of 'umbilicus,/ fattened on mornings like this as on a mother's blood', a connection she has not witnessed before between her children. The image is visceral and startling, using as it does the translucent 'rope' which links the unborn child to its mother, and which feeds the child with blood. She doesn't overstate her conviction about the potential power of this sisterly link (it is 'not yet in focus'), but suggests it could yet have the power 'to knock both of you off your balance/ when you least expect it'. And suddenly she places the sisters 'decades hence'. If you are reading this poem out loud, you will notice that this sentence, which began at the start of the fifth stanza, is beginning to seem never-ending; and in fact it doesn't conclude until the final phrase of the poem. In just such a way, the 'rope' of the poem's title is going to have the power to connect the sisters, without curtailment, right through their lives from this time of engaged mutual play until a crisis that is decades away.

For the poem imagines these little girls as grown women with busy lives that are now lived separately from each other, finding that they are willing to drop everything, 'lovers, kids, apartments', in obedience to the flexing of this rope which is now being created. They will find that they do want to 'be there' for their sister in a crisis, and that this will not be because of the bidding of their mother who has raised them (she might be dead), but because they were once able to play together like this. Crucially, the narrator foresees this constraint of love happening, 'but without me watching'.

What's in a name?

If and when I have mislaid my name
and stare at you disconcertingly

let me spend a day parked by Suilven,
perplexed by broken water. Turn

my calendar to the mountain's season,
and set my watch by shadows on the loch.

Forgive me if I lose the reasons that we came
or my gaze clouds in a cod-fish kind of way

or if the name I chose for you eludes me.
I'll still sense mountain, water, love.

Christine De Luca

Christine De Luca is a poet from Shetland who writes both in English and in the Shetlandic dialect. Here she tackles the subject of dementia, something that is increasingly an issue between the oldest generation and their offspring – often themselves in late middle age. We saw in 'Follower' by Seamus Heaney (see p. 29) the disconcerting reversal experienced by the adult narrator, whose ageing father – once the tender carer of a stumbling little boy – now stumbles after him in a confused but persistent way. De Luca's brief poem is remarkable for the way she addresses head-on the prospect that she herself may develop dementia, such that crucial aspects of her

51

own identity, or that of her son, may start to escape her. What does love mean if such a thing comes to pass, and how might it still be expressed and experienced?

Clearly the narrator of the poem is not yet in the grip of cognitive decline, but she has observed it in others and has made the effort of imagination involved in putting herself in this position. This is a remarkably difficult thing to do, even if one has taken the trouble to set up powers of attorney or advance directives about medical treatment. However much we love our offspring, and enjoy the mature adulthood they may have achieved, we desire very strongly to maintain our competence and our independent agency. This is not just about not wanting to be a burden on the next generation; it is a strong resistance to the notion that they will ever be in charge of us, rather than vice versa. And perhaps we cannot bear to contemplate ourselves in a state of dependency, or forgetful of our own reality in a way that our culture finds pitiable or even disgusting. Dementia, more than almost any other human condition, occupies what has been called 'malignant social positioning', and so it is feared more than death itself.

So this poem, in attempting to inhabit dementia, is an exercise in courage, but also a message to the poet's son which is actually rather comforting. Starting 'If and when I have mislaid my name', the poem accepts dementia as the most probable future ahead for this parent and offspring relationship. The very fact that it is addressed announces that the situation will be one that can be dealt with, even if she seems baffled by the relationship and is inclined to 'stare at you disconcertingly'. Indeed, there are some helpful suggestions about how she would like to be treated under such circumstances. And it's not just 'shoot me'. The poem is very brief, but it is both thoughtful and conversational. Consisting of just ten lines that are set out in pairs, the requests she makes carry on from one line to the next in a connected way. It is gentle and apologetic in tone, but carries a deceptive weight of meaning.

If dementia is her lot, she wants to 'spend a day parked by Suilven' – that very distinctive and much-loved mountain range in a remote part of Sutherland. It rises almost vertically from a wilderness landscape of moorland, bog and small inland lochs; its name means 'the lonely mountain' or 'the grey pillar'. One recalls the ballad 'Joy of Living' by Ewan McColl, which bids goodbye to a number of iconic northern hills and mountains that the singer can no longer climb; the list includes 'cloud-bearing Suilven'. The narrator of the poem envisages herself taken by car and parked so that she can see both the mountain and the loch. If her mind is confused, let it be 'perplexed by broken water'. Having lost her grip of ordinary reality and routine everyday time, she asks that, rather than being surrounded by prompts that bring her back to the world which the cognitively competent are inhabiting, she should be granted the right to be in touch with a quite different, much longer timescale: 'Turn/ my calendar to the mountain's season,/ and set my watch by shadows on the loch'. It has been observed that dementia sufferers, particularly those for whom the outdoors and the natural world were always important, can become both serene and happily absorbed when given the opportunity to spend time in that context again.

She then issues an apology for the condition of her future self: her lack of grasp on the sequence of things or the reason for the journey; the 'cod-fish' gaze which is characteristic of the advanced stages of the disease; the loss not only of her own name but 'the name I chose for you'. Recognizing that this stage of forgetfulness may come to pass, she nevertheless asserts that she will 'still sense mountain, water, love'. The changelessness of the ancient landscape and the unchanging loving regard of her son who has taken her there are still going to be available to her. And this is borne out by observation of dementia sufferers. The loss of the names of their dearest relatives does not necessarily preclude their capacity to sense that they are loved.

This is a brief and beautiful love poem from a mother to her adult son; one which may become relevant but which needs to be written now, just in case this is what comes to pass.

GROWN-UP LOVE

The poems in this section include those that would usually appear in a book of 'love poems' as that term is normally understood: poetry that addresses the adult search for a partner who is committed and offers a kind of love that in some ways echoes the intimate and unconditional love we received (or, at least, needed) when we were an infant. But now it is offered reciprocally between equal partners; that is the dream. Of course it includes erotic connection, or the longing for it; but it is about much more than that.

Many classic love poems celebrate that first heady excitement which accompanies falling in love, perhaps just before, or at the very start of a sexual relationship that is much more than casual. There is an electric tension, and limitless expectations of the beloved and what this relationship will do to transform your life. This kind of love may feel as if its importance transcends the sexual connection, even while it arises from it. Somehow the oceanic feelings of infancy find themselves recreated afresh in the safe arms of another adult who seems to see you and know you as you have never been fully seen and known before. There may be a sense of fulfilment of your very identity; the relationship can seem to matter more than anything else in the world. Lovers can feel as if the bonds of mortality and time simply do not apply to them ('Strawberries', p. 59; 'River', p. 68; 'Story of a Hotel Room', p. 72; 'The Sun Rising', p. 76; 'Bride and Groom Lie Hidden for Three Days', p. 80; 'Slumber-Song', p. 85).

But many forms of passionate love between grown-ups may exist that do not quite fit into this definition. It is possible to experience a profound sense of being in love (often in youth) where the feelings and desires are never actually announced, or a relationship pursued. Though never tested, this love may become an ideal that permeates the whole of life ('Song: I Hid my Love', p. 64). Human beings may, when they face shared danger as comrades in war, forge an intense connection which is as significant and lasting as any love affair. Difficult to speak of back in civilian life, its meaning may transcend the death under fire of one of the comrades ('Angel Hill', p. 93).

And, of course, that stage of ecstasy, of 'no impediments' between the couple, never does last. For one thing, though passionate erotic love declares that it is not 'Time's fool' ('Sonnet 116', p. 98), the fact is that even the most enduring love will end in the death of one party. The price of deep love is deep grief ('The trick', p. 89). And erotic love, expressed or repressed, does not always go well or end well. Powerful feelings are not inevitably reciprocated, and the pain of rejection is built into the risks of love ('The More Loving One', p. 102). Love and desire that are thwarted by an unresponsive beloved can turn into hatred and a wish for revenge ('Behold love', p. 106).

If passionate love does mature into a solid lifelong commitment, it moves on from the early excitement into a daily care, respect, and attention to the details of living together that, over time, truly builds up each person in the relationship, and the lasting power and beauty of the connection between them. The last two poems of the section ('Atlas', p. 110, and 'Scaffolding', p. 114) speak of this kind of enduring love between a couple. Apparently humdrum and understated, and attentive to what is being done rather than what is being felt, they witness to what it takes to embody the heady promises of early passion within the reality of mortal life together.

Strawberries

There were never strawberries
like the ones we had
that sultry afternoon
sitting on the step
of the open french window
facing each other
your knees held in mine
the blue plates in our laps
the strawberries glistening
in the hot sunlight
we dipped them in sugar
looking at each other
not hurrying the feast
for one to come
the empty plates
laid on the stone together
with two forks crossed
and I bent towards you
sweet in that air
in my arms
abandoned like a child
from your eager mouth
the taste of strawberries
in my memory
lean back again
let me love you

let the sun beat
on our forgetfulness
one hour of all
the heat intense
and summer lightning
on the Kilpatrick hills

let the storm wash the plates

Edwin Morgan

This exquisite little poem about desire manages to convey electric adult excitement while focusing almost solely on an innocent activity – slowly and luxuriously sharing plates of strawberries on a hot and sultry day. In its vividly realized detail, we see and feel how grown-up desires take their root from the frank appetites of the children we once were, with our capacity to surrender to the world freshly and to taste how delicious are its simple pleasures. It is no coincidence that the narrator describes his beloved in his arms as 'abandoned like a child'. This heightened sensitivity, and the capacity to 'let go' together are the hallmarks of erotic passion.

Edwin Morgan was a Glaswegian, teaching for many years at the university and enjoying several honours as one of the foremost Scottish poets in the twentieth century. His poetry has an appealing accessibility, and combines raw freshness with a subtle kind of discretion. It was not until he was 70 that he came out as gay, announcing that all his work was written from that perspective. But it is only on close inspection that we realize that the poem itself has offered no internal clues as to the gender of either of the lovers – unless the crossed forks imply something by their overlapping sameness. Yet the poem contains a powerful sense of specific, mutually attracted bodies, with a hint of sexual pressure: 'your knees held in mine'; there is nothing abstract about what is going on. So the text makes itself available to any reader to inhabit, whatever their gender or preference.

The poem is written as a single sentence, lacking in all punctuation including a full stop at the end. There are just a couple of pauses towards the end, expressed in blank lines, perhaps to suggest the points where speech had to cease, or for which there are no words. So it would be possible to read the poem in a breathless way, but my feeling is that it should be taken slowly, with the shortness of each line offering time to wait briefly before the next detail of what happened on 'that sultry afternoon', as if the narrator is actually calling up memories while he speaks. The style is conversational, as if to a long-term lover about the early days of their love, or to that beloved in imagination (now departed for whatever reason) as if he were there to be reminded. It is clear from the opening lines that this is a vivid memory, which has become saturated with the romantic significance of the encounter. 'There never were strawberries/ like the ones we had.' They are remembered as unparalleled: because this was a crucial 'first time'; because no experience of eating (or loving) afterwards ever came up to them; or the poet may be just mocking himself, by implying that the strawberries' perfection is imaginary, like the mis-remembered perfect summers of childhood.

Having established these exquisite, if idealized, fruits as the overarching symbol of glorious intimacy – and there is indeed nothing quite like succulent strawberries at the height of their fruiting season on a very hot day – the poem sets the rest of the scene with just a few telling details. The intense heat has thrown open the French windows; the soon-to-be-lovers are squatting on the step, knee to knee; the plates are blue and the half-bitten fruits are 'glistening'. The juices are running because they are dipping them in sugar; this was a common practice in the days before selective breeding of strawberries ensured added natural sugar to suit contemporary tastes. Strawberries of that era were never bland, so when you dipped them in sugar there was an exciting combination of tartness and intense sweetness together. And they were only available during their short summer season: an evanescent luxury deserving total focus and appreciation.

But, as they eat, the lovers are 'looking at each other/ not hurrying the feast/ for one to come'. There is a lovely grace inherent in this steady, unhurried gaze between them. The slow savouring of the strawberries honours the importance of the simple pleasures of eating; everything is noticed, enjoyed and remembered in retrospect, rather than simply forming a trivial prelude to the main event. It also suggests that the lovemaking, though eager, will not be greedy but tender and appreciative. As the narrator recalls 'the taste of strawberries' returning to him on his lover's mouth, the memory comes full circle; the detail lodges in his heart and mind till this day, wishing the love could be repeated.

At the end of the poem the narrator moves back into the present tense, as if reliving that afternoon in memory. Brilliantly, the word 'forgetfulness' is used to convey the most important part of the memory. At this point we are reminded of how hot it was, and realize there was a storm brewing, with 'summer lightning', and we get the only detail of where this all took place, 'the Kilpatrick hills'. Somehow that one name makes you believe in the factual reality of this encounter.

The last line is stunning. Perhaps a sudden summer downpour is a slightly cinematic cliché for conveying a consummation of love. But suggesting it via a humorous thought about tackling the washing-up of the abandoned but unforgotten strawberry plates is brilliant: 'let the storm wash the plates.'

Song: I Hid my Love

I hid my love when young while I
Couldn't bear the buzzing of a fly;
I hid my love to my despite
Till I could not bear to look at light:
I dare not gaze upon her face
But left her memory in each place;
Where'er I saw a wild flower lie
I kissed and bade my love good-bye.

I met her in the greenest dells,
Where dewdrops pearl the wood bluebells;
The lost breeze kissed her bright blue eye,
The bee kissed and went singing by,
A sunbeam found a passage there,
A gold chain round her neck so fair;
As secret as the wild bee's song
She lay there all the summer long.

I hid my love in field and town
Till e'en the breeze would knock me down;
The Bees seemed singing ballads o'er,
The flyes buzz turned to Lion's roar;
And even silence found a tongue,
To haunt me all the summer long;
The riddle nature could not prove
Was nothing else but secret love.

John Clare

Song: I Hid my Love

Of course, intimacy may be much longed for but never achieved. This poem by John Clare, an underrated working-class poet of the nineteenth century, carries a powerful charge of romantic yearning, even when the relationship it seems to be about may never have gone beyond the platonic.

Clare, who lived and worked on the land in rural Northamptonshire, had a passionate connection with the natural world which was founded on the deep and practical experience of the working labourer, not some city-based idyll. He also had lifelong romantic complications with a variety of women, including his long-suffering wife and mother of his children, Patty. But throughout his poetry the figure of Mary Joyce, the daughter of a local farmer, whom he met and played with as a boy, but never had the courage to woo explicitly, came to represent the purest form of romantic longing of his life. Adolescence is a time when new, profound adult feelings can emerge with piercing intensity, but are embarrassingly hitched to maximum social awkwardness. At the same time, for Clare the connection with Mary seems never to have been complicated by the complexities or routines that an ordinary relationship that is actually pursued inevitably involves. So the feelings for her became unforgettable; perhaps we have all been there. What seems to have happened is that Mary became a sort of 'Muse', and the feelings for her transferred on to many later encounters. Jonathan Bate, in his biography of Clare, quotes a little poem scribbled on the back of a letter draft when Clare was about 40, and it is telling:

> I loved thee, though I told thee not,
> Right earlily and long,

65

Thou wert my joy in every spot,
My theme in every song.

And when I saw a stranger face
Where beauty held the claim,
I gave it like a secret grace
The being of thy name.

And all the charms of face or voice
Which I in others see
Are but a recollected choice
Of what I felt for thee.

The penultimate line about 'recollected choice' may contain a pun on Mary's surname, Joyce. Certainly she became his symbol for the kind of joy that love can bring.

'I hid my love' is apparently an artless ballad, but it is a skilful evocation of deep, unreciprocated adolescent passion, set in the context of the adult narrator's perception that the youthful bashfulness on display is also rather funny. The narrator is aware that the obsessive youthful secrecy about love meant that this love was never consummated or quite possibly never even announced, so came to nothing for the young lover: 'I hid my love to my despite'. The poet manages to interweave the boy's feelings for the object of his passion with his involvement in the natural world. Not only did he 'dare not gaze upon her face', but he 'Couldn't bear the buzzing of a fly'. Perhaps this is an image of hyper-sensitivity, or of a boy feeling that the ordinary sounds of nature (hardly unfamiliar to him) had now become either insistent reminders of his love or accusations about his cowardice in failing to announce it. Whatever the 'flyes buzz' represents, it has ludicrously become a 'Lion's roar' by the last stanza; perhaps the lad just feels infuriatingly helpless to speak; even insects have more of a voice than he does.

There is much talk of kissing: the breeze, which 'kissed her bright blue eye' and later practically blew the boy over; the bees who 'kissed and went singing by' (later apparently managing to sing actual love ballads); the boy himself who seems to apply his lips to sadly fallen flowers. But there is no actual kissing of the girl. The second stanza creates a stunning glimpse of a girl's neck, where a sunbeam seems to have surrounded it with a gold chain as she sits in the summer woods. But was the girl actually there, or is this a constructed scene arising from the adolescent imagination, as he 'left her memory in each place' (while avoiding real, face-to-face interactions)? It seems very unlikely that the girl herself was in the woods and 'lay there all the summer long'. But in his heart she did.

And yet somehow, with all the humour and exaggerated sentiment, the poem contains something powerful and enduring about the impulse towards grown-up love. Even such youthful fervour, untested as it is by reality, cannot be discounted. It does genuinely lie at the heart of what fires us throughout life, and which fuels poetic expression of that impulse: 'And even silence found a tongue.'

River

Down by the river, under the trees, love waits for me
to walk from the journeying years of my time
     and arrive.
I part the leaves and they toss me a blessing of rain.

The river stirs and turns, consoling and fondling itself
with watery hands, its clear limbs parting and closing.
Grey as a secret, the heron bows its head on the bank.

I drop my past on the grass and open my arms,
     which ache
as though they held up this heavy sky, or had pressed
against window glass all night as my eyes sieved
     the stars;

open my mouth, wordless at last meeting love
     at last, dry
from travelling so long, shy of a prayer. You step from
     the shade,
and I feel love come to my arms and cover
     my mouth, feel
my soul swoop and ease itself into my skin, like a bird
threading a river. Then I can look love full
     in the face, see
who you are I have come this far to find, the love of
     my life.

Carol Ann Duffy

The desire for a meaningful, eternal 'love of my life' runs very deep and funds a good deal of our popular culture and music. For this very reason, it takes considerable skill to make a poem that expresses this profoundly romantic dream in an original way, such that anyone would be happy to give the text to an adored new beloved as a love poem. Carol Ann Duffy is exceptionally gifted at writing about this stage of a relationship, although she is also clear-eyed about addressing, in other works, how love goes wrong. She has the capacity to refresh situations and phrases that have become clichés, enabling us to enter them anew.

This is not a love poem of youth. The narrator of this poem has a 'past', and she comes to this love 'from the journeying years of my time'. The scenario the poem creates is that of a romantic assignation down by the river, and the image of the winding, ceaselessly moving river echoes the journey of the speaker towards her beloved. There is something both calm and erotically intense about the tone and pace of the poem, which is divided into unrhymed stanzas of three long lines each.

It is hard to know whether the journey from the first to the last verse takes up just the time it takes to go down to a river, or implies days, seasons or even years of travel. It isn't quite clear what the weather is doing or how the light is falling. Initially there is 'a blessing of rain', later there is a 'heavy sky' and the memory of night-time stars, then it seems to be hot and sunny, as 'You step from the shade', and finally there must be full daylight as love is looked 'full in the face'. Perhaps these changes subtly imply the length of the internal, psychic journey that must be undertaken before the speaker can bring herself to 'arrive'. It is not so much that love is hidden but that the narrator has far to go before she is ready to perceive and receive it.

The conviction of the presence of love, though, is there from the start: 'Down by the river, under the trees, love waits for me.' But the speaker has to take an action and go forward to search for love. There is a beautiful harbinger of future bliss as she parts the leaves 'and they toss me a blessing of rain'. This is both accurate about what wet leaves do if you plunge into the undergrowth, and it effectively leads us directly to the sinuous, mysterious river where the encounter is to happen. The river is practically auto-erotic in its motions 'consoling and fondling itself/ with watery hands, its clear limbs parting and closing'. This image speaks of the longings and loneliness of the poem's narrator so far. It's not mysterious what she wants, and yet there is something secret and sacred about such desire. The heron 'bows its head on the bank' in a stance that suggests the accurate shape of the still bird but also the possibility of prayer.

The central stanza of the poem is the turning point which enables the speaker to become ready to receive what love has to offer – and it seems to be about ceasing to strive for it, to let go of anxiety or the desire to control events. She has to 'drop' her past on the grass and open her arms (by now we are in an opening or glade in the woods which admits of grass and sky). She is aware of her arms aching 'as though they held up this heavy sky', or as if she had been desperately pressing them 'against window glass all night as my eyes sieved the stars'. That remarkable word 'sieved' suggests starey-eyed insomnia and unhappiness, as well as the tiny pinpricks of stars in the night sky.

The fourth verse focuses on her mouth, 'wordless at last' (this from a poet), thirsty and dry from travel. You expect the longed-for word 'kiss' to emerge, but instead we get 'shy of a prayer'. Finally the beloved approaches, but interestingly it is not 'you' but love itself that comes to her arms and covers her mouth. As this stanza ends, it does not end but demands to be carried on, as she feels her soul 'swoop and ease itself into my skin, like a bird/ threading a river'. Thus comes that extraordinary sense of total integration of body, mind and soul which falling profoundly in love can convey. The image of the bird encompassing, almost stitching together a river by darting from bank to bank, links back beautifully with the restless, self-reflexive character of the river earlier in the poem. Only now, when she feels capable of looking love 'full in the face', can she start to explore and name the actual individual who has become the love of her life.

Story of a Hotel Room

Thinking we were safe – insanity!
We went in to make love. All the same
Idiots to trust the little hotel bedroom.
Then in the gloom . . .
. . . And who does not know that pair of shutters
With the awkward hook on them
All screeching whispers? Very well then, in the gloom
We set about acquiring one another
Urgently! But on a temporary basis
Only as guests – just guests of one another's senses.

But idiots to feel so safe you hold back nothing
Because the bed of cold, electric linen
Happens to be illicit . . .
To make love as well as that is ruinous.
Londoner, Parisian, someone should have warned us
That without permanent intentions
You have absolutely no protection
– If the act is clean, authentic, sumptuous,
The concurring deep love of the heart
Follows the naked work, profoundly moved by it.

Rosemary Tonks

Human beings have, over time, engaged in myriad sexual arrangements, which, between adult partners, has often involved equality, reciprocity and deep love – but by no means always. Commitment, sex and love have always been separable, and the modern world is no exception to this.

Indeed, sexual activity for its own sake, without any intention of continuing intimacy, has, since the social revolution begun in the 1960s, become 'normal' in Western society, including for women. (The advent of the contraceptive pill offered women, for the first time, certain protection from pregnancy, arising from their own choice.) Rosemary Tonks' poetry tends to address the excited decadence of that period: 'In sharp contrast with the traditional, well-behaved, dry, self-deprecation verse being published at that time by most of her English contemporaries, her poetry was declamatory, bold, spirited, extravagantly and exuberantly sensuous, a hymn to sixties hedonism.'[4] (Interestingly, she later seems to have rejected what once she celebrated; she converted to a form of fundamentalist Christianity and severed her connections with the world of modern culture.)

This poem, however, reflects what seems to be an adulterous relationship. It is certainly secretive and illicit, since the partners have chosen a rather seedy hotel room as the place for their encounter. The poem starts with that insouciant 'devil-may-care' attitude that can characterize the belief that sex is just sex and has (given adequate protection) no consequences. It appears that the only consideration is the necessary secrecy. 'Thinking we were safe' is purely about whether or not the participants will be found out, and the reader has the impression that the betrayal they might experience from the 'little hotel bedroom' is that it is just not anonymous enough. It is clear that both partners are well practised at just this sort of assignation. The drawbacks of such a cheap, perhaps Parisian, hotel are apparently known to everyone, as they seek to ensure privacy: 'who does not know that pair of shutters/ With the awkward hook on them'. Perhaps the dire nature of the bedroom adds to the arousal, just because it is a case of slumming it. The sexual encounter proceeds according to the reductive ideology of the period. Having mentioned making 'love', in fact the brisk description of what they did stresses that it was simply an act of determined mutual consumption – 'acquiring one another/ Urgently!' An afterthought to the urgency is to describe the sex as a sort of polite hospitality, 'just guests of one another's senses'.

However. The shock of the poem as it proceeds is summed up by Daisy Goodwin, who remarked, 'This poem should be read by anyone about to embark on an affair thinking that it's just a fling. It is much harder than you know to separate sex from love.'[5] The second half of the poem follows a similar form to the first half – ten lines that offer a profound reversal of the expectations set up in the first ten lines. The narrator repeats the thought that they were 'idiots to feel so safe', but for reasons that completely undermine all their previous assumptions about what they were doing. The sexual activity that was all about being so free from consequences that they held back nothing turned out to be 'ruinous', as the narrator confesses with a rueful irony. The nature of the pleasure that turned into ecstasy left them both with 'absolutely no protection' against the treacherous entry of the one who simply hadn't been invited to the occasion – 'The concurring deep love of the heart' that 'Follows the naked work'.

The last three lines of the poem are quite beautiful in their tenderness and self-exposure. As we know, it is hard to write about sex without becoming wincingly embarrassing, as the

74

wrong balance is struck between daring explicitness and too much information. Tonks achieves her stunning statement with an intriguing series of adjectives – words that are not normally found together, but here reverberate with each other: 'clean, authentic, sumptuous'. And then that use of the gentle but decisive word 'concurring' to describe a movement of the heart, rather than an agreement made with the mind. The heart 'Follows' (note the emphatic placing of this word); and what it follows is 'the naked work'. This is a spare, powerful, serious way of referring to sex, which is normally thought of only as pleasure. The heart, although ambushed by love, is not helpless or seduced, but has to admit that it is, in some irreversible way, fully engaged by this encounter that was supposed to be shallow, 'profoundly moved by it'.

'Without permanent intentions' it appeared that safety was secure because neither party intended the other to be trapped into an ongoing commitment. But they were not in fact 'safe'. They have not been found out. They were not struck by guilt, or a sense of responsibility. They have been undone by love itself. The lovers have suddenly shifted from inhabiting a tawdry little hotel into an entirely different place.

The Sun Rising

Busy old fool, unruly sun,
    Why dost thou thus,
Through windows, and through curtains, call on us?
Must to thy motions lovers' seasons run?
    Saucy pedantic wretch, go chide
    Late school-boys, and sour prentices,
  Go tell court-huntsmen, that the King will ride,
  Call country ants to harvest offices;
Love, all alike, no season knows, nor clime,
Nor hours, days, months, which are the rags of time.

    Thy beams, so reverend, and strong
    Why shouldst thou think?
I could eclipse and cloud them with a wink,
But that I would not lose her sight so long:
    If her eyes have not blinded thine,
    Look, and tomorrow late, tell me,
    Whether both th'Indias of spice and mine
  Be where thou left'st them, or lie here with me.
Ask for those kings whom thou saw'st yesterday,
And thou shalt hear, All here in one bed lay.

    She is all states, and all princes, I,
    Nothing else is.
Princes do but play us; compared to this,
All honour's mimic; all wealth alchemy.
    Thou sun art half as happy as we,
    In that the world's contracted thus;

Thine age asks ease, and since thy duties be
To warm the world, that's done in warming us.
Shine here to us, and thou art everywhere;
This bed thy centre is, these walls, thy sphere.

John Donne

Perhaps the most famous of Donne's bedroom poems, 'The Sun Rising' captures brilliantly that stage of erotic passion when it dominates and suffuses all other aspects of the lovers' perceived reality. Magnificent, transformative and deeply energizing to the parties involved, its claims are of course a glorious delusion, since this stage is strictly temporary. Even at the time of its strongest grip, we know that the expectations generated by this kind of love are wild exaggeration. But it is so powerful, and so self-justifying, that we long for this experience and will often seek it repeatedly, with a new partner. What Donne achieves in this poem is to hold together a simultaneous celebration of this semi-divine, passionate state of being in love and a humorous awareness of its grandiose absurdity. But the humour in no way undermines the beauty and compelling power of the lovers' joy.

The poem is spoken as if from the bed itself, just as the first beams of the rising sun fall on it. The man curses the sunshine as a 'Busy old fool' – an ageing busybody (either a voyeur or a spiteful, disapproving gossip) who is peering through the window pane, and even through the curtains, to see what the young lovers are doing. The whole poem is a one-sided disputation between the man and the sun. Beginning with his objection to its outrageous interruption of the lovers' business, it covers a startling range of large claims: who controls times and seasons – you or us? Where is the treasure and the power in this world located – across the regions where you shine each day or right here in this bed? What do your world-warming duties matter anyway? We are the whole world, so just warm us and the job is done. And so he argues himself in stages, from wanting the sun not to arrive, to imperiously demanding that it stop right here and never depart. Love's megalomania is completely absurd and yet wholly recognizable and endearing.

So, the first stanza addresses the question of time. Lovers, apparently, are not subject to the ordinary demands imposed by the passing of time, which the progress of the sun bears witness to. 'Lovers' seasons' work on a totally different timescale, which the boring, quotidian world is unaware of. The narrator challenges the sun (so pedantic about its routine habits) to chase up all the other, unimportant people who have deadlines and jobs and places to get to: 'Late schoolboys', 'sour prentices', 'court-huntsmen'. The latter would be court servants, no doubt kept busy until a late hour the previous evening, whose job, if 'the King will ride', is also to make pre-breakfast arrangements for aristocratic pursuits. It is not only these poor mortals who are dismissed by the poem's narrator; even the way we calculate the passing of time, 'hours, days, months' are scorned as 'the rags of time'. But love dwells in the exalted place of eternity; it 'no season knows, nor clime'.

The second verse mocks the very power of the sun as it scans the world. What is so special about sunbeams? The lover could 'eclipse' them just by winking. (His power, we see, is celestial in its scope and grandeur.) The only reason he doesn't do this is he doesn't want to take a single moment from gazing at his beloved. The poem then makes a seamless shift to considering her power instead of his. Her eyes are likely to have blinded the sun himself, they have such beauty. (We are reminded of that sonnet by Shakespeare that deliberately sends up these traditional, exaggerated comparisons by starting: 'My mistress' eyes are nothing like the sun.'[6]) Then he instructs the sun to check during the day whether the finest of the world's treasures of spice and gold 'Be where thou left'st them, or lie here with me'. And all the kings the sun visited – still in their kingdoms, or here in this bed?

This preposterous conceit leads smoothly on to the lover's tremendous assertion: 'She is all states, and all princes, I,/ Nothing else is.' It is of course an image based on triumphantly patriarchal and colonial assumptions about women and men and what their joining in erotic passion could mean. But many readers will still resonate to that sense that, compared with this passion, 'Nothing else is'; and indeed that political power, honour and wealth are fake goals by comparison. The verse ends with the lover patronizing the sun, now conceived as someone deserving of lighter duties because of advanced age, and assures him that the lovers *are* the whole world. Absurd as it is, this proposition captures precisely the familiar demands of this kind of love, that it be treated as having an importance beyond any other consideration:

> Shine here to us, and thou art everywhere;
> This bed thy centre is, these walls, thy sphere.

Bride and Groom Lie Hidden for Three Days

She gives him his eyes, she found them
Among some rubble, among some beetles

He gives her her skin
He just seemed to pull it down out of the air and lay it
        over her
She weeps with fearfulness and astonishment

She has found his hands for him, and fitted them
        freshly at the wrists
They are amazed at themselves, they go feeling all
        over her

He has assembled her spine, he cleaned each piece
        carefully
And sets them in perfect order
A superhuman puzzle but he is inspired
She leans back twisting this way and that, using it
        and laughing, incredulous

Now she has brought his feet, she is connecting them
So that his whole body lights up

And he has fashioned her new hips
With all fittings complete and with newly wound
        coils, all shiningly oiled

Bride and Groom Lie Hidden for Three Days

He is polishing every part, he himself can hardly
      believe it

They keep taking each other to the sun, they find they
      can easily
To test each new thing at each new step

And now she smoothes over him the plates of his
      skull
So that the joints are invisible
And now he connects her throat, her breasts and the
      pit of her stomach
With a single wire

She gives him his teeth, tying their roots to the
      centrepin of his body

He sets the little circlets on her fingertips

She stitches his body here and there with steely purple
      silk

He oils the delicate cogs of her mouth

She inlays with deep-cut scrolls the nape of his neck

He sinks into place the inside of her thighs

So, gasping with joy, with cries of wonderment
Like two gods of mud

Sprawling in the dirt, but with infinite care

They bring each other to perfection.

Ted Hughes

Ted Hughes' poem 'Bride and Groom Lie Hidden for Three Days' continues the theme of the transcendent power of erotic love at its zenith. It was originally part of a mythic sequence written at a time of great creativity in Hughes' life, in 'Crow: The Life and Songs of the Crow'. This was inspired by the prints of crows produced by his friend Leonard Baskin, at a time when Hughes was recovering from the suicide of his first wife Sylvia Plath. The project became almost the exploration of a new creation myth, where the hero (or anti-hero) of the narrative is the figure of Crow. Traditionally a 'trickster' in some cultures, Hughes described Crow as the forgotten 'oracular god' of Great Britain. Among his adventures, Crow encounters various female figures, culminating in a 'hag' who eventually is transformed into a beautiful naked woman. 'Bride and Groom' is the song that celebrates this moment. However, the story of Crow was never finished by Hughes, since, when he was working on it, his second wife also died by her own hand. But we know, from a broadcast the poet made about the sequence about Crow, 'the whole purpose of the thing is to turn him into a man'. So both male and female are transformed and, as the poem claims, brought to perfection.

So, the mythic context suggests a story where both partners are quite literally as yet not fully created in their resplendent, intended forms; but I think the poem is capable of standing alone as a celebration of the astonishing power of sexual love to confer a completeness and confidence that the parties involved may not have experienced in a bodily way before. It manages to refer in great detail to the mutual exploration of each other's bodies without being either pornographic or embarrassing, and it does this by suggesting that each lover is profoundly engaged in creating the other anew, as if for the first time they receive fully working bodies at each other's hands. Lots of the parts that help a body to see, to move and to work as a connected whole are mentioned – not just the erogenous zones or those parts normally regarded as seductive between the sexes.

> She gives him his eyes, she found them
> Among some rubble, among some beetles

The poem's opening is both arresting and amusing; the reader does a double take from the thought of eyeballs rolling among some shiny insects to the realization that the woman had the power to draw the man's gaze away from his current obsession. His effect on her is similarly startling; it is as if she has only just been clothed in her skin as he pulls it from air and lays it over her, making her weep. This beautifully conveys the hypersensitivity of skin that is newly exposed to the beloved, newly touched. Not only does she source his hands for him, but she has 'fitted them freshly at the wrists' like a new pair of gloves. The initiative passes back to the man as his hands feel 'all over her'. But as they do so, instead of highlighting the classic erogenous zones, the poem describes him reassembling the very structure of her body, her skeleton. He cleans each little bone in her spine 'And sets them in perfect order'. This takes superhuman ingenuity, but it enables her to lean and twist, delighted and incredulous. It is a lovely way to describe the arching of the body that comes with arousal and response.

There is a constant back and forth pattern between the woman and the man, as they tenderly supply or sustain each working part. Sometimes it seems to be about discovery ('She has found his hands for him'); sometimes a matter of construction ('He has assembled her spine'); sometimes it is like maintaining a complex machine ('He oils the delicate cogs of her mouth'), or like working on an artistic design ('She inlays with deep-cut scrolls the nape of his neck'). The way the poem progresses reflects the reciprocal caresses that go back and forth, and the delight and astonishment these give.

And so the lovemaking/recreation proceeds: she brings his feet: he fashions her hips; she smoothes the plates of his skull: he ties together her throat, breasts and pit of her stomach; she ties in his teeth: he sets 'little circlets on her fingertips'. And so it goes on. Quite unexpected parts of the body feel themselves complete, and participate in this act of bringing 'each other to perfection'. In Hughes' story of the Crow, this song is the answer to the question, 'Who gave most, him or her?' It is impossible to say.

Slumber-Song

Sleep; and my song shall build about your bed
A paradise of dimness. You shall feel
The folding of tired wings; and peace will dwell
Throned in your silence: and one hour shall hold
Summer, and midnight, and immensity
Lulled to forgetfulness. For, where you dream,
The stately gloom of foliage shall embower
Your slumbering thought with tapestries of blue.
And there shall be no memory of the sky,
Nor sunlight with its cruelty of swords.
But, to your soul that sinks from deep to deep
Through drowned and glimmering colour, Time
    shall be
Only slow rhythmic swaying; and your breath;
And roses in the darkness; and my love.

Siegfried Sassoon

Sassoon is well known as a poet soldier of the First World
War, who, like many others, joined up enthusiastically as
early as possible but became horrified by the realities of war
and began to take a controversial anti-war stance. But he also,
in his only lightly fictionalized memoirs, recreated the sunlit,
romantic Edwardian era which the leisured classes enjoyed
just prior to the outbreak of war. 'Slumber-Song' probably
dates from the very early part of the war. I first encountered
this beautiful sonnet lying in bed in the dark, listening to
Poetry Please on the radio, and it came over as a profound

and loving adult lullaby, spoken by someone deeply in love to his beloved, who is gradually falling asleep next to him in the bed. Sassoon's partners in the first half of his life were all men, so this distinctive love-song is likely to have been written with another man in mind. But its qualities make it a universally available hymn to the intimate and vulnerable experience of falling asleep beside the one you love.

'Sleep; and my song shall build about your bed/ A paradise of dimness.' The image of a compelling song building a safe, heavenly space around the bed conveys the essence of a lullaby, where a parent typically sings to an infant at bedtime. It is a kind of protective spell to calm a child's fears and racing thoughts, and enable it to drop gently into slumber, to the sound of the loved one's voice. Sometimes a lullaby has been accompanied by bedtime prayers and the invocation of guardian angels. (This may explain the 'tired wings', though you would have thought that the tiredness surely belongs with the sleeper.) So I think the poet is evoking the memory of being sung to sleep as a child, with all the comfort that implies.

The poem is a sonnet, with 14 lines, but its shape does not follow either of the classic forms. Instead of having a significant shift in mood or meaning after the eighth line, or moving through a series of four-line stanzas to a concluding couplet, this sonnet maintains a steady, building mood of somnolence, surrounded by love. As such, it beautifully fulfils its declared purpose of encouraging the person to whom it is addressed gradually to fall asleep. There need be no sudden surprises or shifts, no rousing conclusion, for fear of waking the beloved. At least nine of the lines use enjambement, the technique whereby the reader is prevented from pausing at the line end but must continue steadily, without taking a breath, to pursue the thought into the next line ('You shall feel/ The folding'; 'embower/ Your slumbering thought'; 'Time shall be/ Only slow rhythmic swaying'). This usage contrasts strongly with more traditional sonnets that do pause at the line endings, often including full rhymes to emphasize these.

The soporific mood is also generated by the choice of vocabulary, so that soft consonants like 'l' and 'm' predominate, along with long, sustained vowel sounds (such as 'build', 'feel', 'folding', 'hold', 'lulled', 'gloom', 'dream', 'embower', 'slumbering', 'memory', 'glimmering'). Because of these, the reader of the poem almost has to read slowly, with a sing-song tone, even though the enjambement makes the sentence long. Try reading out loud the following, and this becomes clear:

> and one hour shall hold
> Summer, and midnight, and immensity
> Lulled to forgetfulness.

Notice also how the poem reflects that period, just before sleep, when everything that has been present to the wakeful mind begins to blur into one, and the connections between things dissolve and are gradually let go of. For instead of what is actually around, the sleeper will be surrounded by the internal images generated by his dreams. Here, the narrator of the poem promises that these will be beautiful, soothing and protective, like his whole song: 'The stately gloom of foliage shall embower/ Your slumbering thought with tapestries of blue.' You can almost imagine lying beneath leafy trees on a summer day and seeing the complex shadows of the foliage.

At this point, through their banishment from his dreams, there is a hint of what the beloved needs protection from: 'there shall be no memory of the sky,/ Nor sunlight with its cruelty of swords.' There is a sense of exposure and danger in sunlight here, so there may be hints of the war; but the reference is too general to be certain. The poem returns to its soothing encouragement of the descent of the soul into sleep, through 'drowned and glimmering colour' – a strangely evocative phrase, which, with the 'rhythmic swaying', almost suggests an underwater scene. It is an oceanic metaphor for that strange entry into unconsciousness to which the mysterious everyday fact of needing to sleep brings each of us, for reasons still not fully understood. The masterful, soporific voice of the loving narrator has succeeded in bringing the beloved out of the grip of time, and reality is reduced to his sleeping breath, the scent of the summer 'roses in the darkness' and, of course (though mentioned explicitly for the first and only time), the protective power behind this effective incantation, 'my love'.

The trick

In a wasted time, it's only when I sleep
that all my senses come awake. In the wake
of you, let day not break. Let me keep
the scent, the weight, the bright of you, take
the countless hours and count them all night through
till that time comes when you come to the door
of dreams, carrying oranges that cast a glow
up into your face. Greedy for more
than the gift of seeing you, I lean in to taste
the colour, kiss it off your offered mouth.
For this, for this, I fall asleep in haste,
willing to fall for the trick that tells the truth
    that even your shade makes darkest absence
      bright,
    that shadows live wherever there is light.

(After Shakespeare, Sonnet 43)

Imtiaz Dharker

Imtiaz Dharker is a Pakistan-born British poet, raised in Glasgow and having strong ties with Wales and India. Her wide-ranging sympathies and observant, conversational style make her poetry accessible to many, including those who might not normally engage with the sonnets of Shakespeare. When Dharker made a YouTube recording of this poem for GCSE students, she described it as a love poem, which she had been trying to write for some time in response to a particular dream, but it wouldn't come right. Then, when she decided to use the formality of the sonnet form (in particular paying a certain homage to Shakespeare's Sonnet 43), she was able to write the poem. The poet adheres closely to the classic form of a Shakespearean sonnet, having three four-line stanzas which rhyme on alternate lines, followed by a concluding rhyming couplet that asserts the truth or insight which the poem's argument has built.

'The trick' seems to be about the pursuit of a recurring dream concerning a dearly beloved lover who has died (Dharker's own husband died in 2009 after some years of living with cancer). It reminds us that the eventual price of deep love is always deep grief. The poem is in no way a slavish copying of Sonnet 43 in a modern form; indeed it isn't clear that the two poems are about the same thing at all. Shakespeare's poem, as Dharker has pointed out, 'is such a perfect sonnet of absence and presence, presence in absence'.[7] But I think the beloved addressed within it is an idealized living person, to whom the lover is making his appeal, seeking to persuade him to come back in reality and not just in dreams:

> All days are nights to see till I see thee,
> And nights bright days when dreams do show
>   thee me.

Dharker comments that the poem plays tricks on the mind with light and shade, with words that look and sound the same but make cunning grammatical shifts. Indeed it does, but her own poem takes that 'trick' and explores a more profound and painful area of experience, which is that of actual bereavement.

Literally unable to see him in her waking life, the narrator of this poem describes how he is present, vividly, in dreams, and how that in turn brings her to life. This dream presence is therefore a 'trick' she is deliberately willing to 'fall for'.

Dharker's poem plays with double meanings, grammatical shifts and deliberate paradoxes from the start. 'In a wasted time' sets us firmly within the landscape of grief, with its sense of time-wasting greyness and boredom. And for the narrator, perhaps, there is also the sense of being 'wasted' – destroyed or laid waste by the impact of bereavement, loss and point-lessness. By contrast with her daytime life, 'it's only when I sleep/ that all my senses come awake.' The depression of grief has blunted all of her sense impressions: nothing feels vivid, nothing matters. But in sleep they return. A heartbreaking pun (a classic technique of Shakespeare's) comments on this paradox about coming 'awake': 'In the wake/ of you, let day not break.' The 'wake' is the powerful backwash made by a departing ship (and the lover has indeed departed), but by echoing the word 'awake' it also means the beloved appar-ently alive and awake, awakening all her sense. 'Let day not break' is the classic prayer of the grief-stricken, who returns each morning from powerful dreams to the hard reality of the beloved's unchangeable absence.

The narrator uses wonderfully hard, concrete words to describe the reality of the beloved which she longs to retain; each of them linked to a different sense (smell, touch, vision), each of them ending in the hard stop of a 't' consonant: 'Let me keep/ the scent, the weight, the bright of you.' She makes a wordplay on her determination to 'take/ the countless hours and count them all night through', as if taking the desolation of grief by the throat and insisting that her terrible loss by day shall be made good at night, as if she can choose the lover's presence in her dreams. And initially it seems that she can. The image of the husband coming to 'the door/ of dreams, carrying oranges that cast a glow' is arresting and distinctive. Perhaps based on an actual memory, the intense, shining colour of the fruits underline the acute awareness of her senses that is available only in the dream world.

In her dream she presses for more, for the satisfaction of another sense. The word 'Greedy' at the start of the sentence about leaning to kiss her beloved suggests that she has gone too far. The desire for a kiss is emphasized by the wordplay of 'off' and 'offered': 'kiss it off your offered mouth', but we are not told whether she does indeed experience the taste of him. Our own experience of dreams that dissolve and vanish at the crucial moment would suggest probably not. Instead, there is a full stop and a repeated cry of yearning: 'For this, for this, I fall asleep in haste.' This is the trick; she knows it, but she cannot resist longing for it every night. And so the poem reaches its own painful play on dark and light, that love itself creates the pain of grief: 'even your shade makes darkest absence bright,/ that shadows live wherever there is light.'

Angel Hill

A sailor came walking down Angel Hill,
He knocked on my door with a right good will,
With a right good will he knocked on my door.
He said, 'My friend, we have met before.'
    No, never, said I.

He searched my eye with a sea-blue stare
And he laughed aloud on the Cornish air,
On the Cornish air he laughed aloud
And he said, 'My friend, you have grown too proud.'
    No, never, said I.

'In war we swallowed the bitter bread
And drank of the brine,' the sailor said.
'We took of the bread and we tasted the brine
As I bound your wounds and you bound mine.'
    No, never, said I.

'By day and by night on the diving sea
We whistled to sun and moon,' said he.
'Together we whistled to moon and sun
And vowed that our stars should be as one.'
    No, never, said I.

'And now,' he said, 'that the war is past
I come to your hearth and home at last.
I come to your home and hearth to share
Whatever fortune waits me there.'
    No, never, said I.

'I have no wife nor son,' he said,
'Nor pillow on which to lay my head,
No pillow have I, nor wife nor son,
Till you shall give to me my own.'
    No, never, said I.

His eye it flashed like a lightning-dart
And still as a stone then stood my heart.
My heart as a granite stone was still
And he said, 'My friend, but I think you will.'
    No, never, said I.

The sailor smiled and turned in his track
And shifted the bundle on his back
And I heard him sing as he strolled away,
'You'll send and you'll fetch me one fine day.'
    No, never, said I.

Charles Causley

Some kinds of passionate love resist being pinned down. This remarkable little ballad by Charles Causley succeeds in being completely compelling and poignant, while utterly defying the power of the reader to decide finally what it is about.

Causley was a poet rooted in Launceston, Cornwall, and he lived there, in his mother's house, virtually all of his life. His passion for the region was clear, but he was more reserved about his private life.

The poems too both reveal and conceal. With a surface simplicity that belies the many layers of truth beneath them, many of his strongly rhymed and metred poems take the form of sea shanties or ballads. Some of his poems have been set to music and sung as such by Jim Causley (a distant relative), which highlights the emotional power of the form. Causley often used it when he was dealing with his experience of service with the Royal Navy during the war, a period of life which had a profound and formative effect on him. He was stationed for a time at Scapa Flow on Orkney, and experienced terrifying naval battles as they sought to protect the arctic convoys from enemy attack. He saw comrades drown and ships go down. After the war, Charles wrote in a personal letter:

> I think the event that affected me more than anything else in those years was the fact that the companion who had left my home town with me for the Navy in 1940 was later lost in a convoy to Russia. From the moment I heard this news, I found myself haunted by the words in the 24th chapter of Matthew: 'then shall two be in the field, the one shall be taken and the other left.' If my poetry is 'about' anything it is this.[8]

'Angel Hill', I believe, emerges out of this apocalyptic experience, and is about a kind of haunting of a survivor of that period, by one of his closest comrades on board ship, who did not make it home. (Causley lived near an actual street called Angel Hill.) Like many ballads, it simply tells a story in a direct and jaunty fashion, with a repeated refrain at the end of each stanza that comments on what has been said and done so far. But this refrain is a repeated statement of denial on the part of the singer, and indeed it is the only thing that the singer/narrator says throughout: '*No, never,* said I.' What the denial means in each verse depends on what has gone before, but you have the sense of a cheerful visitor, the sailor, encountering an increasingly desperate and stonewalling narrator. He refuses to recognize the sailor; to acknowledge the bitter, vivid memories of their friendship under fire; to remember the vows they made to each other; to integrate his memory of his friend into his current life; or to agree that there might come a day when he would want to meet him again. The refusals may be about a kind of homoerotic subcurrent, which the narrator resists acknowledging, but we cannot know. Nevertheless, the detailed elements of the memory suggest passionate intensity (the 'sea-blue stare' that becomes 'like a lightning-dart'; the loud laughter, the smile and the singing; the piercing memories of shared hardship) – images that can never be suppressed, however hard the narrator may try. Perhaps those of us who have never experienced it cannot fathom the intense comradeship of war, which is forged by imminent danger and may throw the whole of life and death into a sharp perspective that is impossible to communicate to folk back home, and is thus painful to recall.

One of the remarkable features of the poem is the huge contrast in tone between the visiting sailor, who is cheery and feisty throughout, and the sullen narrator whose only emotion appears to be deep frozenness: 'My heart as a granite stone was still.' The sailor anticipates a welcome but when he does not receive it he remains firmly confident that this will eventually change: 'My friend, but I think you will.' What is the significance of this encounter? The power of the poem is the ordinary tone in which this disturbing event is retold, and the clue is in the title. This return of the man he loved has been a wholly disconcerting visit from an angel (maybe even the angel of death) to a numbed survivor who does not want to think about these things. The poet, of course, is the creator of both the poem's voices.

Sonnet 116

Let me not to the marriage of true minds
Admit impediments; love is not love
Which alters when it alteration finds,
Or bends with the remover to remove.
O no, it is an ever-fixèd mark,
That looks on tempests and is never shaken;
It is the star to every wandering bark,
Whose worth's unknown, although his height be
    taken.
Love's not Time's fool, though rosy lips and cheeks
Within his bending sickle's compass come;
Love alters not with his brief hours and weeks,
But bears it out ev'n to the edge of doom.
    If this be error and upon me proved,
    I never writ, nor no man ever loved.

William Shakespeare

This sonnet is so famous that it is the one you know when
you aren't familiar with any of the others, so beloved is it of
wedding organizers. It is the classic poem about idealized
romantic love, capturing precisely the absolute conviction of
the passionate lover, who is certain that he is addressing his
soul mate, and that their love will never falter, change or be
destroyed, whatever challenging circumstances may arise. It
seems a perfect choice to accompany the exchange of lifelong
vows, and many have invested this poem with profound sig-
nificance thereby.

However, it is always tricky to know exactly what tone a poem of Shakespeare's should be read with, and arguably there is a subtext here which is working to counteract the poem's strong surface assertions. Inspection of the rest of the sonnets suggests that this author has some complicated things to say about erotic passion and its variability, about ambivalence, about the ravages of time, and indeed about more than one lover. Some of the poems are addressed to a 'dark lady', but others, including this one, are to a young man. It is true that the implied narrator of this sonnet is totally convinced of the unchangeability of his passion, but this narrator may be unreliable. Love's hotly asserted promises, and love's actual behaviour, may sometimes be at odds.

To start with, we need to reconsider the well-known phrase 'marriage of true minds'. Marriage, essentially, is a union of bodies ('with my body I thee worship'). Though minds may also be involved, they are not normally placed at the fore-front in this way. Could the narrator have a problem with the male body of his beloved? (Legal same-sex marriage is of very recent origin.) And then the phrase, 'Admit impediments'; this is taken directly from the marriage service, where anyone who knows any 'just impediment' to the proceedings is required to declare it. Why is the narrator announcing that there are no impediments? To do so is precisely to intro-duce the idea that impediments do exist. Is this 'marriage' of true minds taking place in reality or only in some idealized longing on the part of the speaker?

The next famous assertion, 'love is not love/ Which alters when it alteration finds', also deserves careful inspection. At one level, this is true. 'Love' that evaporates the moment any problems arise, or when the lover comes across a more enticing potential partner, was probably never love in the first place. Commitment should mean stickability. However, real love does also alter through time, according to what happens. Parenthood is a classic exercise in finding that some of the ways you used to love your child need to be dropped as they mature, and quite other ways of expressing your love or willingness to support them need to be adopted. In erotic love between adults, material things can alter, which call forth necessary alterations. One of you may become ill or disabled, and the way love is expressed between the couple may need to change dramatically. One of you may betray the other, or become controlling or violent, or may simply abandon the relationship. For your love not to change under these circumstances is hardly healthy. Even in the best scenario possible, one of you will die first. Love may continue, but grief does and should change things profoundly.

Then we have the classic 'ever-fixèd mark' – that is, a sailor's mark, a lighthouse to provide certainty of direction in the middle of a storm. The 'star to every wandering bark' would be the pole star, which seems to maintain its position always as being reliably due north. This would have been a crucial fixed point to every marine traveller of Shakespeare's era. The assonance of 'star' and 'bark' (and the earlier 'mark') hold the lines together brilliantly. As the poet Don Paterson puts it, it makes 'the contrast between the star's fixity and the boat's wandering even more sharp'.[9] The next line means that, while the star's distance may be measured by a sextant, its value, or 'worth', is inestimable – like love, he implies.

Here Shakespeare performs a traditional shift between the first eight lines and the next six, starting again with an arresting phrase that everyone can now quote: 'Love's not Time's fool.' It is a bold but, to my mind, unconvincing assertion. We are all the fools of Time; we are mortal; bodies age and die. And indeed, the poem immediately produces a powerful clause which completely contradicts the first statement: 'though rosy lips and cheeks/ Within his bending sickle's compass come'. The image of Time's harvesting blade taking out 'rosy lips and cheeks' is excruciating, and the enjambement at the line end seems to emphasize the unending scope of Time's reach. Love does not necessarily save even youth from this reality. For me this is the place where the poem touches the ground and moves the reader's heart; we wish, against the evidence, that Time did not have this power.

The final four lines, however, retreat into the unreal assertions of the first part of the poem. We are back with the fantasy that Love is not affected by the mere 'brief hours and weeks' of Time, and is headed, changelessly, for 'the edge of doom'. Really? Even marriage vows are, realistically, only binding 'till death do us part'. The poem is an anatomy of the wish-fulfilment fantasy of a lover who is consumed with the idea of a changeless human love. Sadly, it *is* an 'error'.

The More Loving One

Looking up at the stars, I know quite well
That, for all they care, I can go to hell,
But on earth indifference is the least
We have to dread from man or beast.

How should we like it were stars to burn
With a passion for us we could not return?
If equal affection cannot be,
Let the more loving one be me.

Admirer as I think I am
Of stars that do not give a damn,
I cannot, now I see them, say
I missed one terribly all day.

Were all stars to disappear or die,
I should learn to look at an empty sky
And feel its total dark sublime,
Though this might take me a little time.

W. H. Auden

If we cannot be sure of the tone of the sonnet by Shakespeare, it seems that we can be quite sure, from the first two lines of this poem by Auden, that we are well into the realm of heavy irony. It appears that the narrator is in love, but that his feelings are not reciprocated. Gazing at the stars in true romantic fashion, he discovers that it really doesn't quite work when you try to impute to the realm of nature some of the passions that possess the human heart, and so the whole subject receives a thorough debunking. (Compare the non-ironic lover in Donne's 'The Sun Rising', where the whole of creation is invoked to do his bidding.)

Auden's poem is so heavily metred and rhymed that it is almost doggerel, which emphasizes the absurdity of the lover's speculation about the stars. The bitter colloquial phrases that a disappointed suitor may use to express the indifferent attitude of the object of his devotion are simply comical when applied to 'stars that do not give a damn', whose view is that 'for all they care, I can go to hell'. Of course stars are completely unaffected by the longings of any particular individual on earth; however moved we are by their existence, it is a category mistake to imagine that reciprocation is on the cards. The narrator has enough self-awareness to turn the fantasy around and admit that, however much he loves the starry night sky, 'I cannot, now I see them, say/ I missed one terribly all day.'

This convoluted speculation about passionate stars is the narrator's way of trying to deal with the pain of his rejection: first by claiming that it isn't so bad ('indifference is the least/ We have to dread'); then by pointing out that no one likes being loved with a passion we cannot return; then by arguing that things he loves, like stars, he doesn't really miss when they aren't in sight; and finally by claiming he could get used to the absence of stars, if they simply weren't there. But of course his agony, comical as he makes it appear, is not about stars, but about precisely the one individual human being among the countless millions on this earth whom he has indeed been missing terribly all day, but who has effectively told him to 'go to hell'.

Auden has on other occasions used the technique of expressing intense emotional pain through the medium of brittle, absurdist little rhymes whose exaggerations and irony are suddenly burst asunder by a few lines of plain speaking or painful lyricism that allows us to see an exposed and suffering male psyche beneath the clever joking it has used for self-protection. His poem 'Funeral Blues', which took audiences by storm when it was used in the film *Four Weddings and a Funeral*, is one of these. Into a ditty which appears to be depicting ironically the absurd public acts of mourning prescribed for a fallen dictator (stopping all the clocks, sky-writing the news of his death, issuing traffic police with black gloves), a heart-stopping stanza is inserted. It speaks directly to those who have been bereaved of a lover, of whatever gender, who 'thought that love would last for ever', but were proved wrong.[10]

In this poem, too, we are given an unforgettable couple of lines, phrased almost as a prayer, which many disappointed lovers have clung to, along with the shreds of their dignity: 'If equal affection cannot be,/ Let the more loving one be me.'

The final stanza of the poem is both bleak and arresting, as the narrator contemplates in his imagination a night sky that lacks all stars, and claims that he could learn to view such an empty sky 'And feel its total dark sublime'. This creates an image of galactic emptiness, alongside a knowledge of humanity's capacity to generate meaning and significance out of literally nothing. It bears witness both to the broken heart's desolation and to its resilience and determination to heal. However, the narrator admits, 'this might take me a little time'; a classic stiff-upper-lip understatement, which belies the pain he is suffering.

Behold love

Behold, love, thy power how she despiseth,
My great pain, how little she regardeth.
The holy oath, whereof she taketh no cure
Broken she hath, and yet she bideth sure
Right at her ease and little she dreadeth.
Weaponed thou art and she unarmed sitteth.
To thee disdainful her life she leadeth,
To me spiteful without cause or measure.
    Behold love.

I am in hold: if pity thee moveth,
Go bend thy bow that stony hearts breaketh,
And with some stroke revenge the displeasure
Of thee and him, that sorrow doth endure,
And, as his lord, thee lowly entreateth.
    Behold love.

Thomas Wyatt

A disappointed and rejected lover does not always react with valiant efforts to get over the pain and adopt a different perspective on his suffering, like the narrator in Auden's poem 'The More Loving One'. Sometimes revenge is on the agenda; this is where hostile stalking may be born.

For Thomas Wyatt, writing in the sixteenth century, there was a whole tradition of writing about erotic love which acknowledged the dark side of the god Eros. Then (as now, ironically, on Valentine's cards) he was depicted as a young, curly-headed god with sharp arrows – the better for piercing the hearts of the unwary with passionate attachment to someone who might or might not feel the same in return. Eros was understood to be not only exciting and enlivening in his influence over humanity, but also potentially terrible and destructive. In the classical tradition inherited from Greece and Rome, Eros was prayed to, not just to open the heart of the beloved towards the one praying but sometimes to punish the indifferent or the hard-hearted in his own distinctive way. Let her too be wounded by the agonizing darts of unreciprocated desire.

The poem is a 'rondeau', which is a poem of ten or thirteen lines with only two rhymes used throughout, and with the opening words used twice as a refrain. This tight, disciplined form, which makes the reader take it quite slowly, induces a sense not of calm but of considerable menace. It starts with an invocation to Love, asking him to 'behold' the demeanour of the woman who is the heartless object of the speaker's affections. It is clear from the following lines that this word 'Behold' is an invitation not just to look but to assess and condemn. The careful grammatical inversions in almost all of the clauses in the first stanza place great emphasis on the subjects of the verbs: 'thy power', 'My great pain', 'The holy oath'. There is a solemnity here that almost sounds like a formal series of accusations in a court of law, which comes to its climax at the start of the fourth line, when the beloved's crime is named explosively at the start of the line: 'Broken she hath'.

The second half of each line subsides into verbs with soft, so-called 'feminine' endings ('despiseth', 'regardeth', 'taketh', 'dreadeth'). These are used to great effect as they set up the hard, emphatic words that start the next line, powerfully conveying the sense of pain and protest in the voice of the speaker. It is as if he cannot forgive the woman, not just for rejecting him but for seeming to be so blithely unaware of her effect on him or (in his mind) of the legitimate demands of Love: 'and yet she bideth sure/ Right at her ease'.

Then the speaker turns his gaze on the figure of Love himself, and again reverses normal grammatical order, this time to highlight that Love can be violent and not just a benign blessing: 'Weaponed thou art and she unarmed sitteth.' It is an implied threat, via the figure of Eros, which emphasizes in a disturbing way the sheer vulnerability of his beloved. I have to say that this poem reverberates unpleasantly with echoes of modern situations of domestic violence, where one partner who has been rejected meditates or even enacts horrible revenge on the other. The speaker seeks to justify his thoughts by pointing out the bad behaviour of the beloved: 'To thee disdainful' (that is, not appropriately respectful of the divine power of the god Eros); 'To me spiteful without cause or measure'. The latter is perhaps always the view of the self-absorbed lover who fails to grasp why he falls short or why a relationship has had to end. The stanza ends as it began, with the phrase 'Behold love', this time drawing our attention ironically to the shortcomings and faithlessness of the one with whom he once shared love.

The second verse draws attention to the lover's pain and then spells out his prayer. 'I am in hold.' I think this means that the lover is paralysed with pain and cannot move on. He begs for 'pity' from the god, but what he pleads for is not release from his own feelings but agony for her too: 'Go bend thy bow that stony hearts breaketh'. He acknowledges the power of Eros as 'his lord'; but his lowliness and deference to Love's power can only long for 'revenge', not actual mercy, either for himself or for his beloved. And then comes the final 'Behold love', like a repeated refrain. Here, it almost feels as if the speaker briefly stands back from his accusation and prayer, making a bitter comment on the place that his feelings have brought him to. When erotic love goes wrong, it is terrible and unforgiving indeed.

Atlas

There is a kind of love called maintenance,
Which stores the WD40 and knows when to use it;

Which checks the insurance, and doesn't forget
The milkman; which remembers to plant bulbs;

Which answers letters, which knows the way
The money goes; which deals with dentists

And Road Fund Tax and meeting trains,
And postcards to the lonely; which upholds

The permanently ricketty elaborate
Structures of living; which is Atlas.

And maintenance is the sensible side of love,
Which knows what time and weather are doing
To my brickwork; insulates my faulty wiring;
Laughs at my dryrotten jokes; remembers
My need for gloss and grouting; which keeps
My suspect edifice upright in the air,
As Atlas did the sky.

U. A. Fanthorpe

The final two poems in this section explore something of what can happen when an erotic partnership does not go wrong, but by contrast becomes a long-term, committed relationship that can be depended upon. If love fulfils the promises it set out with, and actually lasts until death divides the lovers, what are its characteristics?

U. A. Fanthorpe was a poet who only began to write and publish poetry in later life, and she enjoyed a partnership of many decades with another woman poet. The poems they wrote for each other speak of deep love, which is both erotic and profoundly comfortable and pragmatic. Fanthorpe herself often reveals deep feelings through attention to the ordinary but crucial matters of everyday life.

Here she is using the classical, mythological figure of Atlas, who according to legend was one of the Titans who fought against the Olympian gods and lost the battle. Zeus then condemned him to hold up the sky for all eternity. (Some classical depictions show him shouldering the globe instead of the whole cosmos, and it is from this that his name has been given to any collection of world maps, as well as to the Atlantic ocean.) It is a heroic task, and in some ways the comparison made in the poem between this and the upholding of the ordinary tasks of living creates an absurdity. And yet sometimes the business of maintaining life in a household does feel like an Olympian task, especially when illness or frailty or depression are around – or just a temperament that isn't well adapted to the ceaseless demands of administration or household repair.

'There is a kind of love called maintenance.' This low-key title for a kind of love initially undersells its significance; it does not sound as important as the agonies and idealism of a grand passion. But as the poem proceeds, listing the range of relatively small matters that have to be attended to if life is to be comfortable and hospitable, we realize that this is in fact a paean of praise to the partner who takes the trouble to focus on detail. This kind of love involves checking and remembering (renewing insurance and car tax, paying the milkman, keeping a handle on the household budget, making dental appointments); it involves knowledge, and takes action accordingly (how to use WD40, when to plant bulbs). And mixed in with this humdrum 'to do' list is a care for people as well as a desire for a smoothly running household (letters are answered, postcards are sent to the lonely, and trains are met). The poem points out that this attentiveness – very much the unsung, traditional province of women, usually wives or mothers – is not insignificant, but is what keeps in place the 'permanently ricketty elaborate/ Structures of living'. This is 'Atlas', and the definition is not absurd.

The second half of the poem almost seems to begin again, reaffirming that 'maintenance is the sensible side of love'. Again there is a similar list of what this sensible love does, this time apparently focusing not on paperwork or minor maintenance jobs but on the bigger tasks associated with the structure of a house: issues about the weathering of brickwork, faulty wiring, worries about dry rot, or the perennial need for refreshing the paintwork or the grouting. But then the reader notices that each item on the list is preceded by the word 'my': 'my brickwork', 'my faulty wiring', 'my need for gloss or grouting'. The metaphorical nature of this list is given away by 'Laughs at my dryrotten jokes', which tenderly indicates what a loving partner does to prop up her companion's self-esteem. (At the same time it doesn't rule out the sense that the house's structural needs are no doubt being remembered as well.)

So this fascinating little love poem makes, in its self-deprecating way, a huge claim: namely that it is this very unseen love that ensures her own continuance as a functioning person, 'which keeps/ My suspect edifice upright in the air/ As Atlas did the sky'. It points out that enduring love is a matter of what you do, not of what you promise. And you do it day in day out; and it is through attending to the small matters of ongoing maintenance – of the shared household and of the personhood of your partner – that you embody what lifelong promises can mean.

Scaffolding

Masons, when they start upon a building,
Are careful to test out the scaffolding;

Make sure that planks won't slip at busy points,
Secure all ladders, tighten bolted joints.

And yet all this comes down when the job's done,
Showing off walls of sure and solid stone.

So if, my dear, there sometimes seem to be
Old bridges breaking between you and me,

Never fear. We may let the scaffolds fall,
Confident that we have built our wall.

Seamus Heaney

Seamus Heaney is another poet who enjoyed a decades-long life partnership, to his wife Marie, also a poet. This short poem appears to be a testament to the solidity of that relationship, and, like the previous poem by Fanthorpe, it is apparently undramatic, dwelling on a single extended metaphor that has to do with the construction and maintenance of a household.

The poem simply consists of five rhymed couplets, and yet it manages to be conversational in tone, like a comfortable exchange between lifelong partners who know one another very well. Its pace is slow and reassuring, matching the sense of care and attention to detail that must be engaged if a building is to be constructed safely. It begins by focusing on the scaffolding that needs to be in place, to prepare for the work of construction of the wall. The reader's eyes are directed to matters that non-specialists would probably overlook: the 'busy points' where planks may suffer slippage; the need to secure ladders; checking that bolted joints have not worked loose. Scaffolding is not the building itself, only the preparation for it – the safety structure that will allow permanent building to take place. Often it has to stay in place for an unconscionable length of time, while snags are dealt with. To the outsider, the scaffolding is the only aspect of the building that is open to view for ages.

Indeed, in the poem, the process of creating the real thing is not dwelt on at all; it is just what is suddenly revealed when 'all this comes down when the job's done'. Eventually, the temporary structure which was the scaffolding, but which perhaps everyone had got used to, is simply brought down and stacked away, as the 'walls of sure and solid stone' are revealed. The speaker then addresses his wife, applying the metaphor to their marriage. It is, on reflection, a beautiful and subtle comparison. The early years of a lifelong relationship may well need to involve careful negotiation and attention to pressure points between the partners. Slippage or even catastrophe cannot be ruled out, and some matters need to be consciously agreed and regularly checked. However, this structure of relating turns out to be a matter of scaffolding only, creating together the safety structure that will allow them to do the true psychic building of the marriage beneath it, protected by the scaffolding but not open to inspection by others until it is ready to be shown.

Written after many decades of marriage, the poem shows awareness of aspects of the relationship that seem to be changing, and these are the areas that the speaker of the poem identifies as scaffolding only, possible to be discarded when the deep work of bonding has been achieved. We do not know what kind of 'bridges' the speaker is referring to, which are now 'breaking between you and me', but anyone who has experienced long-term partnership can hazard a guess. Often the raising of children in a marriage can be a source of powerful connection between the partners, but this task comes to an end. Grown-up offspring may keep in touch, but they no longer hold together the home they grew up in. As partners age, patterns of lovemaking and sleeping together can change. Poor health or joint pain can affect libido or make sexual activity a challenge; sleep becomes more fragile and partners sometimes find they need to sleep apart in order to achieve a good night.

But the love that survives the passing of years and the process of ageing is not just a gentle afterthought to the period of initial connection and passion. It is the real thing – the solid wall rather than the preparatory scaffolding. This is beautifully brought out by the connection between the fourth and fifth couplet. Instead of pausing on the second line as the other couplets have done, the line about bridges breaking does not itself break, but carries on over the gap to the triumphant reassurance, 'Never fear'. After a sudden admission to hospital following a fall, Heaney famously texted his wife as he was dying, sending this same message, this time in Latin, 'Noli timere'. Effectively the poet's last words, they echo the message that angels bring to human beings throughout the

Bible, when glorious news about the hidden reality of the divine, or about resurrection, is to be revealed.

And so the long-term lover reassures his beloved that the changes can be accommodated, not regretted, and this is the final glory of love when its enduring beauty and solidity can be shown to the world: 'We may let the scaffolds fall/ Confident that we have built our wall.'

GOD AND THE HUMAN HEART

Everyone knows Christianity declares that 'God is love'. And the corresponding charge, that we should love God in response, remains at the centre of all Christian worship today.

> 'You shall love the Lord your God with all your heart, and with all your soul, and with all your mind, and with all your strength.'
> (Mark 12.30, RSV)

It is so familiar that we do not necessarily notice how strange this commandment is. We can be commanded to obey, to submit, or to do certain things, or to refrain from doing certain things (as in the classic phrase, 'Thou shalt not'). But how can we be commanded to 'love'? Our culture tends to see love as something that cannot be commanded, that just happens to us, whose power exceeds our own willpower or reason. Yet here we are asked to immerse every part of our being in the activity of loving God, as if it were a choice; and this flows out into love of others and ourselves. How can this be done?

There is a wealth of poetic tradition in English, exploring the love of God for humanity and the response of the human heart, and in this book it is possible to include only a tiny selection. When we are talking of the love of God, it is axiomatic that the language we use will be highly metaphorical. Perhaps any intense love always leads us into a kind of speechlessness, but here it is inevitable. There is a powerful strand of devotional poetry that takes its imagery from the remarkable biblical love poem, the Song of Songs. This inspired centuries of monastic contemplation on the soul's passion for God, here reflected in Roy Campbell's translation of the poem by the Spanish mystic John of the Cross. In English, devotional love poetry sometimes depicted the relationship from God's point of view, for example the traditional carol about the incarnation, 'Tomorrow shall be my dancing day', with its repeated refrain: 'This have I done for my true love.'

Beyond the monastic tradition, there began to be a wave of interest in spiritual introspection and meditation on the individual's personal relationship with God within his or her own life's journey. Directed boldly towards God, but without the polite formality of traditional liturgical prayers, the contemporaries Donne and Herbert wrote with extraordinary candour about their passion for God, but also their anger, resistance and frustration, as they sought to find meaning in life and comfort for their souls.

The age of reason, and the rise of the Enlightenment, also saw the growth of a passionate form of enthusiastic

Christianity which in many ways prefigured the Romantic movement in poetry. Charles Wesley succeeded in creating hymn texts that are very singable in public worship but that also work as private devotions for ordinary people without an expensive classical education – all you need is familiarity with the Bible. They combine elegant, reasoned theological argument with the bold passion of a human lover.

In the Victorian era, we find some extraordinary, visionary women poets, both churchgoing and church-resisting. This was an era where many women writers, in their different ways seeking to transcend the constraints society imposed on them, began to make their voices and their distinctive, passionate spirituality heard in the public domain. Christina Rossetti and Emily Dickinson each in their very different ways explore their sense of the divine with reference to the landscape. Dickinson in particular brings that exploration to the very edges of language. Rossetti's work shows knowledge of the great scientific discoveries of the Victorian age. Gerard Manley Hopkins, working within a committed religious vocation, was also a contributor to the scientific observations of his contemporaries, and his experimental poetry breaks all sorts of formal boundaries, while, like Herbert and Donne, exploring and celebrating his love for God.

The religiously sceptical twentieth century saw the great Welsh poet R. S. Thomas, who, while pursuing a priestly vocation all his life, nevertheless produced a volume of work charting the deep difficulties of faith and prayer. It is also a century where, for many, agnosticism was the only possible choice. E. J. Scovell's poetry witnesses to the authentic spiritual struggle that this can involve.

Finally I have included two poets who are still living and writing on religious themes, the Shetlandic poet Christine De Luca and Rowan Williams. I have chosen poems that approach our human search for God somewhat indirectly, through inhabiting key biblical stories around the major themes of incarnation and resurrection. They enable us to see some of the consequences of choosing to respond to God's love: insight, transformation, purpose – and also getting rather more than we bargained for: our lives turned upside down.

Song of Songs 5.2–8

I sleep, but my heart waketh:
it is the voice of my beloved that knocketh, saying,
Open to me, my sister, my love,
    my dove, my undefiled:
for my head is filled with dew,
    and my locks with the drops of the night.

I have put off my coat;
    how shall I put it on?
I have washed my feet;
    how shall I defile them?

My beloved put in his hand by the hole of the door,
    and my bowels were moved for him.

I rose up to open to my beloved;
    and my hands dropped with myrrh,
and my fingers with sweet smelling myrrh
    upon the handles of the lock.

I opened to my beloved;
    but my beloved had withdrawn himself, and was
        gone:
my soul failed when he spake:
I sought him, but I could not find him;
    I called him, but he gave me no answer.

The watchmen that went about the city found me,
they smote me, they wounded me;
   the keepers of the walls
   took away my veil from me.

I charge you, O daughters of Jerusalem,
   if ye find my beloved,
that ye tell him,
   that I am sick of love.

Authorized Version of the Bible (KJV)

This is a short section from an ancient series of love poems in Hebrew, rather startlingly found in the Old Testament, the Song of Songs. This is because it is a key text which underlies a powerful tradition of Christian meditation on the love of God, which takes its imagery not from the events of the life of Jesus but from this highly erotic poetry, spoken in the voices of two lovers. It was a text much beloved in monastic circles. Highly influential writers like Origen (third century) and Bernard of Clairvaux (twelfth century) preached extensively on the poem as showing forth the relationship of passionate desire between God and the soul. Not surprisingly, it was seen as a text that was not for the novice, the immature or the worldly. What is perhaps surprising is that in our generation, the poem is largely ignored for spiritual purposes.

The Authorized Version (often called the King James Bible or the King James Version) was published 1611, but under-lying it was decades of fervent and controversial work in the sixteenth century to render the Scriptures into English, thus making them available to the common reader. There was great

124

anxiety about doing this, and the Song of Songs was exactly the sort of biblical text that learned people worried would fall into the wrong hands. Yet the translators here did not hold back on the earthiness of the text they were working with. Indeed, I have decided to use the King James Version precisely because it conveys more powerfully the eroticism of the Hebrew than modern versions tend to do. You can have a lot of fun looking up parallel translations of verse 4. The Hebrew is definitely referring to a visceral reaction to the touch of the lover: the word for 'inward parts' which were 'in a ferment' is definitely well below the belt. This area was understood to be the seat of emotions, and the term is sometimes used of God being moved. So the KJV translation, 'my bowels were moved for him', is spot on. Of course this expression has an amusing modern meaning and would need to be rendered differently, but what we notice in more modern renderings is how smartly the emotion travels higher up the body or turns into something much less concrete and more romantic and soft focus: 'my heart was thrilled within me' (RSV); 'my inmost being yearned for him' (NRSV); 'I trembled to the core of my being' (NJB); 'my heart began to pound for him' (NIV).

But it is worth thinking about why this poem sequence, manifestly about erotic love, has had such power to speak to Christian tradition about God's desire for us and our longing for God. Many readers will be familiar with the luscious praise songs, redolent with images of the natural world in spring, which the lovers speak to each other – these are often picked out for wedding readings. But the overriding metaphor that keeps returning is that of passionate searching – a search that is nearly but not quite ever fulfilled. At one moment the lover is at her door, his hair damp with the dews of the night, begging her to 'open to me'. There is reluctance, expressed in the lovely detail about not wanting to put her feet, freshly washed to get into bed, on to the dirt floor again. The verses about the door latch and hands that are dripping with sweet-smelling myrrh are extraordinary, and it seems that she is also meaning the door of her body. It is as if she is seduced into a full readiness and longing for an intimacy which is then incomprehensibly withdrawn. There are two firm verbs in Hebrew announcing that the beloved 'had withdrawn himself, and was gone', and I think it is this experience, of being intimately called, and then apparently abruptly abandoned by God, that the monastic tradition found so compelling. Their vocation to devote their lives to God was sometimes overwhelming and entrancing, but then quite often (and perhaps quite suddenly) an emotional desert. The approach of God to the human heart is rapidly succeeded by the requirement to undertake a lifelong search oneself, seeking to satisfy the longings God has stirred up.

The term translated here as 'my soul failed' means literally 'my soul went forth'. Suddenly the woman who didn't wish to get her feet dirty on the floor of her room is sallying forth into the streets of the night, encountering danger and violence, having her veil stripped from her. In any generation, this is highly counter-cultural and risky behaviour for a woman, so what we have here is the glorifying, in pursuit of a divine lover, of conduct that society would normally condemn. Following after God is full of risk. Only the exaggerations inherent in erotic passion are sufficient to explain why anyone would do this. She is 'sick of love'; faint with love-longing; desirous of her beloved to the point of sickness and unreason.

Upon a Gloomy Night

Upon a gloomy night,
With all my cares to loving ardours flushed,
(O venture of delight!)
With nobody in sight
I went abroad when all my house was hushed.

In safety, in disguise,
In darkness up the secret stair I crept,
(O happy enterprise)
Concealed from other eyes
When all my house at length in silence slept.

Upon that lucky night
In secrecy, inscrutable to sight,
I went without discerning
And with no other light
Except for that which in my heart was burning.

It lit and led me through
More certain than the light of noonday clear
To where One waited near
Whose presence well I knew,
There where no other presence might appear.

Oh night that was my guide!
Oh darkness dearer than the morning's pride,
Oh night that joined the lover
To the beloved bride
Transfiguring them each into the other.

Within my flowering breast
Which only for himself entire I save
He sank into his rest
And all my gifts I gave
Lulled by the airs with which the cedars wave.

Over the ramparts fanned
While the fresh wind was fluttering his tresses,
With his serenest hand
My neck he wounded, and
Suspended every sense with its caresses.

Lost to myself I stayed
My face upon my lover having laid
From all endeavour ceasing:
And all my cares releasing
Threw them amongst the lilies there to fade.

John of the Cross, trans. Roy Campbell

The sixteenth-century Spanish poem 'Noche Oscura' ('Dark Night') by the mystic St John of the Cross is a remarkable work, here given an equally remarkable translation by the poet Roy Campbell. Campbell manages to reflect almost exactly the rhythm and rhyme scheme and the passion of the original. The poem obviously relies heavily on resonances of the Song of Songs, and indeed on the centuries of monastic tradition which has interpreted the Song as a celebration of the radical way of life pursued by a vowed religious, who is motivated by the sacred 'wound' of love for God. John, who was much loved as a wise and compassionate spiritual director for monks and nuns alike (including the celebrated Teresa of Avila), seems to have written this poem not to stand alone but to accompany the rest of his teaching about the need for the earnest seeker after God to go through first a process of emptying, darkness and purgation. It is from John that we have the expression 'dark night of the soul' – these days often applied to general troubles in life, but then having a specific meaning within the traditional path of spiritual progress.

But the tone of this poem is anything but anguished. It makes a wholehearted use of the erotic imagery of the Song of Songs, while focusing even more on joy and fulfilment than the biblical text does. The one who is the seeker in this poem does encounter and enjoy the divine beloved. The setting, reflecting chapter 5 of the Song, is 'una noche oscura' into which the soul goes out searching. But the English 'gloomy' is not right in tone; there is nothing depressing about the Spanish term. It is simply very dark, and the emphasis is on how the soul is disguised, concealed and unseen in its explorations. The most obvious, literal reading of the poem is that it is indeed about someone riskily sneaking out of a sleeping house to keep a secret assignation with a lover. The protagonist (female, as in the Song) is full of excitement about her daring adventure. This English version emphasizes this aspect: the bracketed lines in the first two verses speak of a 'venture of delight' and a 'happy enterprise'. But they are identical lines, and 'dichosa ventura' means 'happy chance'. Although the narrator of the poem is herself fired up, 'inflamada', and takes action, it is also the case that the sacred moment is given to her. One translation renders these lines: 'Ah, the sheer grace!'

Campbell also varies another pair of repeated lines, the last line of each of the first two verses, which speak of 'mi casa sosegada', and he strongly suggests the sleeping presence of others, whom the soul is escaping from. But I suspect that for John, 'mi casa' (my house) is about a part of himself that he is leaving behind when his soul departs for the secret stair. Underlying this poem is the phrase in the Song, 'I sleep, but my heart waketh' (5.2, KJV), and much was made of this in the mystical tradition. The restless human ego needs to be persuaded to 'sleep', in order for the heart, profoundly in love with God, to be able to sense her call towards her divine lover. The 'house' of the earth-based personality and will needs to be stilled and hushed, before that movement becomes possible. It is a very secret undertaking, done by the heart without any normal prompts or guides, except for the burning sense of love. What John calls darkness, English mystical tradition sometimes calls a 'cloud of unknowing'. This is a place of unknowing that can only be entered by love, and is the only place that God can be approached. Love can somehow know and touch God directly, where all other forms of the human search for knowledge fail and must be abandoned. In verse four, 'no other presence' echoes 'no other light' in emphasizing the primacy of love as the sole means of approach.

The fifth verse is ecstatic in its praise of the holy darkness, more lovely than the dawn. Underlying this may be Psalm 139, which famously asserts that 'the darkness and the light are both alike to thee' (KJV). The great weight of symbolic tradition tends to label darkness as the place of evil and fear, and daylight as the place of safety and beauty. This is no surprise, given how human beings, before the modern era, would have experienced almost total darkness at night, with all its attendant inconveniences and dangers. But here is nothing but joy; it is the place of consummated love, celebrated through all the second half of the poem (I wish I had space to comment on all the following verses, with their sense of the mystical union of the soul with God, imaged in a passionate erotic encounter). The Spanish, with its gendered nouns, leaves English struggling, since it can engage in wonderful, repeated wordplay that suggests transformation and similarity at the same time, as the soul takes on the form of the divine. The night has united 'Amado con amada,/ Amada en el Amado transformada'.

Affliction (1)

When first thou didst entice to thee my heart,
    I thought the service brave:
So many joys I writ down for my part,
    Besides what I might have
Out of my stock of natural delights,
Augmented with thy gracious benefits.

I looked on thy furniture so fine,
    And made it fine to me;
Thy glorious household-stuff did me entwine,
    And 'tice me unto thee.
Such stars I counted mine: both heaven and earth
Paid me my wages in a world of mirth.

What pleasures could I want, whose King I served,
    Where joys my fellows were?
Thus argued into hopes, my thoughts reserved
    No place for grief or fear;
Therefore my sudden soul caught at the place,
And made her youth and fierceness seek thy face:

At first thou gav'st me milk and sweetnesses;
    I had my wish and way:
My days were strew'd with flowers and happiness:
    There was no month but May.
But with my years sorrow did twist and grow,
And made a party unawares for woe.

Affliction (1)

My flesh began unto my soul in pain,
    Sicknesses cleave my bones,
Consuming agues dwell in every vein,
    And tune my breath to groans:
Sorrow was all my soul; I scarce believed,
Till grief did tell me roundly, that I lived.

When I got health, thou took'st away my life,
    And more; for my friends die:
My mirth and edge was lost; a blunted knife
    Was of more use than I.
Thus thin and lean, without a fence or friend,
I was blown through with every storm and wind.

Whereas my birth and spirit rather took
    The way that takes the town;
Thou didst betray me to a lingering book,
    And wrap me in a gown.
I was entangled in the world of strife,
Before I had the power to change my life.

Yet, for I threaten'd oft the siege to raise,
    Not simpering all mine age,
Thou often didst with Academic praise
    Melt and dissolve my rage.
I took thy sweeten'd pill, till I came near;
I could not go away, nor persevere.

Yet lest perchance I should too happy be
    In my unhappiness,
Turning my purge to food, thou throwest me
    Into more sicknesses.
Thus doth thy power cross-bias me, not making
Thine own gift good, yet me from my ways taking.

Now I am here, what thou wilt do with me
    None of my books will show:
I read, and sigh, and wish I were a tree;
    For sure then I should grow
To fruit or shade: at least some bird would trust
Her household to me, and I should be just.

Yet, though thou troublest me, I must be meek;
    In weakness must be stout.
Well, I will change the service, and go seek
    Some other Master out.
Ah, my dear God! though I am clean forgot,
Let me not love thee, if I love thee not.

George Herbert

The seventeenth century saw a blossoming of spiritual intro-spection, in which many religious writers plumbed the depths not just of the Scriptures (now available in English) but of their own life experience, as a source of understanding about God. At the same time, there was an interest in how the English language itself could be well used as a medium for poetry. This may sound obvious, but the language of education was Latin: scholars were taught to translate both out of and into Latin poetry as well as prose. George Herbert was a skilled Latin poet (he became the official Orator at Cambridge University), and the English poetry for which he is now famous was never published during his lifetime. He clearly used his 'versing' as a private way of reflecting on and even negotiating his relationship with God, which he commented provided 'a picture of the many spiritual conflicts that passed betwixt God and my soul'. As such, he gave permission on his deathbed for the poems to be published, in case they could offer consolation for 'any dejected poor soul', and this is why we have the treasure of his verse. While the poems show the careful construction a classical education taught, their vocabulary is remarkably *un*-Latinate, using homely words of single syllables that convey a strong sense of intimacy and honesty.

Herbert consciously rejected the idea of devoting his writing skills to creating love poetry, whether flowery and romantic or frankly erotic, directed to a human lover, fashionable as this was. His dedication to addressing only God, perhaps rather a prissy and puritanical resolve in a young man, nevertheless produced a body of work that became increasingly blunt, self-aware and poignant. And it is interesting that the language of passion or even seduction is not absent: 'When first thou didst entice to thee my heart . . .' The story of his relationship with God begins, and continues, in desire: 'Therefore my sudden soul caught at the place,/ And made her youth and fierceness seek thy face.' But what emerges centre stage is the experience of 'affliction'; Herbert wrote no fewer than five poems with this title. Here, after four verses in which he rejoices in his youthful devotion based on the beauties of creation ('thy furniture so fine'; 'There was no month but May'), he traces the sudden shift, as the realities of adult life kick in. He wrestles with how to deal with his different ambitions, with his deteriorating health, with bereavements that strike, and their consequent griefs and depressions, and with his sense of being stuck in his academic profession; and he challenges God to make sense of his life for him ('what thou wilt do with me/ None of my books will show'). He depicts frustration with himself brilliantly: 'a blunted knife/ Was of more use than I'; 'I read, and sigh, and wish I were a tree.' The poem has the remarkably modern feel of someone in a kind of mid-life crisis, anguished about the life choices still open to him, mining his own life for the source of meaning, rather than just obediently affirming the doctrines and remedies of official Christian faith.

The final stanza is a brilliant summary of the options open to the afflicted Christian soul, as the narrator's demeanour shifts suddenly several times. There are two lines where he reminds himself of his duty to be meek in the face of adversity and testing. Then there is the furious switch to rebellion, deciding to 'seek/ Some other Master out'. Then, just as suddenly, the shift back into the helplessness of his heart's love. The worst imaginable punishment for refusing, as he has just proposed, to love God is precisely finding in himself the inability to do so: 'Let me not love thee, if I love thee not.'

Holy Sonnet XIV

Batter my heart, three-personed God, for you
As yet but knock, breathe, shine, and seek to mend;
That I may rise and stand, o'erthrow me and bend
Your force to break, blow, burn, and make me new.
I, like an usurped town, to another due,
Labour to admit you, but O, to no end.
Reason, your viceroy in me, me should defend,
But is captived and proves weak or untrue.
Yet dearly I love you and would be loved fain,
But am betrothed unto your enemy.
Divorce me, untie, or break that knot again,
Take me to you, imprison me, for I,
Except you enthrall me, never shall be free,
Nor ever chaste, except you ravish me.

John Donne

John Donne was Herbert's older contemporary and was a
friend of Herbert's widowed mother, Magdalen Herbert. The
two men are often contrasted as religious poets. There is some-
times a violence in Donne's tone which is not quite there in
Herbert's (though he has plenty of anger), or perhaps it is that
Donne leaves things unresolved and raw. And as we know,
Donne's 'Holy Sonnets' were preceded by a body of work that
can be startling in its frank delight in erotic pleasure.

There was quite a period in my life when I could not read or
relate to this famous poem at all. An alpha male who has spent
a good deal of his literary life revelling in his robust seduction

techniques now construes his own soul as feminine in relation to God, and seems to be asking to be battered, dominated and raped. ('Ravish' then had a much tougher meaning than its modern one.) Ugh.

But then I heard the setting of this poem by the composer John Adams, in his contemporary opera *Dr Atomic*, which tells the story of Robert Oppenheimer, who was one of the leading scientists involved in the development and testing of the atomic bomb. The hero sings this poem at a key point in the action, just before a test is about to happen. The address of the poem to the 'three-personed God' is perhaps an ironic echo of the name given to the testing of the bomb, Trinity. But it is an appropriate lyric in other ways. Oppenheimer did read widely in poetry and theology (not only Christian theology), and is thought to have been deeply ambivalent about the project he was involved with. Determined to fulfil his duty in seeking to win the war, he was fully conscious of its world-changing violence. Famously, he quoted the line in the Hindu Bhagavadgita, 'Now I am become death, the destroyer of worlds.' Two years after the Trinity explosion, he said, 'The physicists have known sin; and this is a knowledge which they cannot lose.' Hearing Donne's anguished poem again in the context of this man's life and choices made me hear the text quite differently.

As a love poem, it is perhaps the most deeply shocking text in our culture, right from the start. 'Batter my heart'; it is an extraordinary prayer for a violent relationship, and the force of it is immediately contrasted with the gentle verbs of the second line: 'knock' (at the door, like the lover in the Song of Songs), 'breathe', 'shine' (like the dawn), 'seek to mend'.

These actions of course reflect what the narrator knows is the characteristic approach of one who loves, and yet they are listed as a complaint, rather than a paean of praise. Instead, he asks God to display total force: 'o'erthrow me and bend/ Your force to break, blow, burn, and make me new'. The explosive consonant 'b' at the start of the whole poem is repeated here, suggesting hammer blows. In other poems, Donne has shown how one may reconcile oneself to enduring hard times by detecting God's merciful intent within them. 'A hymn to God my God in my sickness' ends: 'Therefore that he may raise, the Lord throws down.' In this poem, such a violence is begged for.

Then one of the two images is introduced, which control the rest of the poem. The speaker conceives his heart as like a town that has been usurped from the power of its rightful ruler. Reason, which should act as a viceroy for God, defending the true best interests of the captured city, is itself held captive 'and proves weak or untrue'. The image resonates with that initial word 'Batter'. God must besiege this city and recapture it; battering rams are called for. We have reached the end of the sonnet's first eight lines, the 'octet', which fully sets out the problem.

The 'sestet' marks a sudden shift in tone, as the voice of the vulnerable lover (rather than the stubborn resister) of God is heard: 'Yet dearly I love you and would be loved fain.' But there is an immediate problem; someone else, the evil one, has claimed her affections instead: 'But am betrothed unto your enemy'. 'Betrothal' suggests not just mutual attraction but willing consent to a binding agreement – undoing a formal betrothal was then almost as hard as repudiating a marriage. The soul has chosen this self-destructive attachment and cannot see, by itself, how to get free of it. So, just as God's force is called on to 'break, blow, burn' the walls of a captured city, so is God asked to 'Divorce me, untie, or break that knot again'. Marriage was virtually indissoluble in Donne's era, so the language is extreme – justified because a partnership with the evil one was certainly not something that God had 'joined together'. The narrator begs to be abducted, prevented from returning to this partnership, and the poem finally brings together both controlling images in a pair of mind-blowing paradoxes: 'for I,/ Except you enthrall me, never shall be free,/ Nor ever chaste, except you ravish me.' To 'enthrall' means to hold in thrall, to imprison; it is interesting that the modern meaning has softened, as with 'ravish'.

And so what I take from this poem now is a violent self-accusation, a cry from the heart of what would today be called toxic masculinity. It is about being unable to respond to God's gentle love with an unambivalent answering heart's desire. Like St Paul (another alpha male), the speaker of this poem laments 'For the good that I would I do not: but the evil which I would not, that I do' (Romans 7.19, KJV).

Open, Lord, my inward ear

Open, Lord, my inward ear,
   And bid my heart rejoice;
Bid my quiet spirit hear
   Thy comfortable voice;
Never in the whirlwind found,
   Or where earthquakes rock the place,
Still and silent is the sound,
   The whisper of thy grace.

From the world of sin, and noise,
   And hurry I withdraw;
For the small and inward voice
   I wait with humble awe;
Silent am I now and still,
   Dare not in thy presence move;
To my waiting soul reveal
   The secret of thy love.

Thou didst undertake for me,
   For me to death wast sold;
Wisdom in a mystery
   Of bleeding love unfold;
Teach the lesson of thy cross:
   Let me die, with thee to reign;
All things let me count but loss,
   So I may thee regain.

Show me, as my soul can bear,
    The depth of inbred sin;
All the unbelief declare,
    The pride that lurks within;
Take me, whom thyself hast bought,
    Bring into captivity
Every high aspiring thought
    That would not stoop to thee.

Lord, my time is in thy hand,
    My soul to thee convert;
Thou canst make me understand,
    Though I am slow of heart;
Thine in whom I live and move,
    Thine the work, the praise is thine;
Thou art wisdom, power, and love,
    And all thou art is mine.

Charles Wesley

Before Charles Wesley, the poetry of the eighteenth century was largely in the grip of neoclassicism, with its heightened and artificial diction, its literary attachment to 'heroic couplets' and its devotion to themes arising from Greek and Latin literature in order to express any emotion: nymphs, shepherds and pagan gods such as Pan or Apollo. Another strand was the cool, rational, detached Enlightenment philosophizing that we find in the work of Wesley's almost exact contemporary, Alexander Pope. By contrast, in the extraordinary and prolific hymns of Charles Wesley, published in the *Hymn Book for the People called Methodists* in 1780, we find the kind of plain language, lyrical experimentation and profound interior exploration of the self that will later be seen in the work of Wordsworth and the other Romantic poets. Charles' brother John wrote in the Preface:

> In these hymns there is no doggerel; no botches; nothing put in to patch up the rhyme; no feeble expletives. Here is nothing turgid or bombast... Here are no cant expressions, no words without meaning ... We talk common sense ... Here are, allow me to say, both the purity, the strength, and the elegance of the English language; and, at the same time, the utmost simplicity and plainness suited to every capacity.

It is like a precursor to the Preface to the *Lyrical Ballads*.

The hymns were aimed at the ordinary person, and gave huge respect to the interior life and feelings of the individual. But these were not an end in themselves; the passion is directed to the relationship with God, reflecting the momentous conversion of the heart which both Wesley brothers experienced in 1738. (This was not a conversion from unbelief to Christianity – both were already ordained clergy – but a shift from a somewhat fearful religious conformity to a joyful sense of being fully loved and accepted.)

This hymn is a beautiful example of the way Wesley combines myriad biblical echoes and stories with a sense of the mystical importance of the heart's passion, all in down-to-earth and homely language. Addressed directly to God, it is as if the speaker is composing himself for a kind of prayer that is about listening, hoping to hear the voice of God in his 'inward ear'. So the poem begins by inhabiting the famous story of Elijah on Mount Carmel (1 Kings 18), where the prophet experiences a whirlwind, earthquake and fire, but senses God not in these dramatic natural phenomena but in a subsequent 'voice of thin silence'. This is Wesley's 'whisper of thy grace', which requires a withdrawal from 'sin, and noise/ And hurry', in order for the heart to be attentive and receptive. We are reminded of John of the Cross' 'casa sosegada'. What the speaker is waiting for is 'the secret of thy love'; it is like the secret assignation of the 'Noche Oscura' (see p. 127).

At the centre of the poem is a stanza that describes the cross and its significance, but in language of considerable economy: 'Wisdom in a mystery/ Of bleeding love unfold'. The carefully chosen term 'unfold' suggests that there are layers of meaning here, which may take at least until death to fully explore and grasp. There are several echoes of St Paul at the end of the verse (Philippians 3.7–8). This is the language of the biblical theology of redemption, but the poem's tone of voice is like that of the passionate lover in the Song of Songs: 'All things let me count but loss,/ So I may thee regain.'

Only after showing the depths of God's love does the hymn move towards self-examination and confession, and even then it asks to be shown 'The depth of inbred sin' only so far 'as my soul can bear'. There is a respect for individual awareness and vulnerability. And the word 'inbred' is brilliant. It is a 'plain' word, but manages to suggest both the traditional doctrine of original sin and a kind of incestuous, self-destructive impulse, or an inner dialogue where the heart dwells fruitlessly on guilt. Then we have the soul asking to be brought 'into captivity' by the one who has redeemed it. In a way, it is similar to Donne's 'enthrall me', but the tone is utterly different, given the gentle probing (not violent battering) of love in this verse. And it is significant what exactly the speaker asks to be made captive. It is not his whole self, or even his lowest impulses, but 'Every high aspiring thought/ That would not stoop to thee'. Wesley is a clergyman, a preacher, and it is precisely his professional pride, his self-aggrandizing achievements that (like St Paul) he wishes to 'count but loss'. The word 'stoop' is superb. Probably we have the image of a falcon here, flying high and refusing to 'stoop' to the wrist of its handler. We would also stoop to a child. Paradoxically, we need to respond to God by moving downwards, earthwards, not in the realm of abstractions. The poem ends with a sense of being finally ready to shift internally, 'Though I am slow of heart'; and once more we are in the realm explored by John of the Cross, with the heart resting in the blissful embrace of its divine lover: 'Thou art wisdom, power, and love,/ And all thou art is mine.'

What good shall my life do me?

No hope in life: yet is there hope
In death, the threshold of man's scope.
Man yearneth (as the heliotrope

For ever seeks the sun) through light,
Through dark, for Love: all, read aright,
Is Love, for Love is infinite.

Shall not this infinite Love suffice
To feed thy dearth? Lift heart and eyes
Up to the hills, grow glad and wise.

The hills are glad because the sun
Kisses their round tops every one
Where silver fountains laugh and run:

Smooth pebbles shine beneath: beside,
The grass, mere green, grows myriad-eyed
With pomp of blossoms veined or pied.

So every nest is glad whereon
The sun in tender strength has shone:
So every fruit he glows upon:

So every valley depth, whose herds
At pasture praise him without words:
So the winged ecstasies of birds.

What good shall my life do me?

If there be any such thing, what
Is there by sunlight betters not?
Nothing except dead things that rot.

Thou then who art not dead, and fit,
Like blasted tree beside the pit,
But for the axe that levels it,

Living show life of Love, whereof
The force wields earth and heaven above:
Who knows not Love begetteth Love?

Love in the gracious rain distils:
Love moves the subtle fountain-rills
To fertilize uplifted hills,

And seedful valleys fertilize:
Love stills the hungry lion's cries,
And the young raven satisfies:

Love hangs this earth in space: Love rolls
Fair worlds rejoicing on their poles,
And girds them round with aureoles:

Love lights the sun: Love through the dark
Lights the moon's evanescent arc:
Same Love lights up the glow-worm's spark:

Love rears the great: Love tends the small:
Breaks off the yoke, breaks down the wall:
Accepteth all, fulfilleth all.

O ye who taste that Love is sweet,
Set waymarks for the doubtful feet
That stumble on in search of it.

Sing hymns of Love, that those who hear
Far off in pain may lend an ear,
Rise up and wonder and draw near.

Lead lives of Love, that others who
Behold your lives may kindle too
With Love and cast their lots with you.

Christina Rossetti

Christina Rossetti's explicitly religious poetry, which makes up more than half her work, puts her firmly in the mainstream Christian tradition, and offers a fascinating insight into how the constraints of Victorian womanhood could interact with strong passions, intellectual force and a very serious approach to the demands of faith.

One of four siblings, including the pre-Raphaelite artist Dante Gabriel (Christina was the model for his famous Annunciation painting *Ecce Ancilla Domini!*), she was home-educated by her mother and her Italian father (a Dante scholar). She was quite a 'stormy' and independent child, and as a girl was no doubt asked to restrain these tendencies.

She wrote and indeed published verses from a young age, and commented later: 'If any one thing schooled me in the direction of poetry, it was perhaps the delightful idle liberty to prowl all alone about my grandfather's cottage-grounds.'[11] Her poetry has a lyrical simplicity which can seem to belie her considerable scholarship and wide-ranging influences, of which the natural world is a powerful one. This was the age of Darwin, and of intense interest in and detailed observation of nature's workings, and how the conclusions of naturalists could be seen to impact on Christian faith.

Although she was close to the pre-Raphaelites, Christina never adopted their free-thinking approach, and was instead a dedicated Anglo-Catholic worshipper, with their traditions of confession, ritual and devotion to the Eucharist. More than once, she turned down suitors on the basis of their religious incompatibility. She was serious about good works, and volunteered at a refuge that offered prostitutes an escape from the streets. She was outspoken against slavery, imperialism and vivisection, and supported raising the age of consent to protect children from sexual exploitation.

Rossetti's poetry often feels quite downbeat and self-accusing, and inclined to write off this life as nothing compared with life hereafter; and this poem is no exception. But once we have battled through the title and first line, we realize that this narrative depression is only the context for a magnificent hymn of praise to divine Love, as it can be perceived in the natural world by those with eyes to see. Immediately we are in an intriguing pattern of three-line stanzas, with a single end rhyme in each. This conveys a dancing rhythm and the impression of childlike simplicity (but you try creating such verse without sounding trite). The narrator seems to be in debate with herself. The proposition to her gloomy self is: 'Shall not this infinite Love suffice/ To feed thy dearth?' Like the psalmist, she bids herself 'Lift heart and eyes/ Up to the hills' (Psalm 121).

God's love is imaged by the touch of the sunlight – beautiful but also literally life-giving – on the whole landscape. Its 'tender strength' warms each nest and 'kisses' the round tops of hills, and causes the plain green grass to grow 'myriad-eyed/ With pomp of blossoms veined or pied'. The response of nature is the kind of wordless praise evoked by the canticle Benedicite from the Book of Common Prayer, and includes here the wonderful 'winged ecstasies of birds'. But then there is a sudden sinister note. Sunlight is beneficial for all things 'except dead things that rot'. The narrator turns this thought into a powerful exhortation to herself: 'Thou then who art not dead, and fit,/ Like blasted tree beside the pit,/ But for the axe that levels it,/ Living show life of Love.' The reference is to a hard saying of Jesus to his disciples (Luke 3.9). She does not allow herself to luxuriate in hopelessness.

After this turning point at the poem's centre, the speaker returns to praise of divine, creative love, moving effortlessly from beautiful echoes of the psalms (for example, Psalms 104 and 147) to a cosmic perspective that understands the earth, with its magnetic polar auroras as only one part of a vast universe: 'Love hangs this earth in space: Love rolls/ Fair worlds rejoicing on their poles,/ And girds them round with aureoles.' It is reminiscent of Dante's praise of 'Love that moves the sun and the other stars', with extra nineteenth-century science. The vast range of Love's reach is shown by contrasts in size ('the moon's evanescent arc' and 'the glow-worm's spark'). But then there is a seamless shift into social contrasts and Love's restless energy for justice: 'Love rears the great: Love tends the small:/ Breaks off the yoke, breaks down the wall'. There are echoes of St Paul's great hymn to love in 1 Corinthians 13 (see p. 184). So we and the speaker herself are left with the challenge to 'Lead lives of Love', fired by this same creative and life-giving force.

My period had come for Prayer

My period had come for Prayer –
No other Art – would do –
My Tactics missed a rudiment –
Creator – Was it you?

God grows above – so those who pray
Horizons – must ascend –
And so I stepped upon the North
To see this Curious Friend –

His House was not – no sign had He –
By Chimney – nor by Door
Could I infer his Residence –
Vast Prairies of Air

Unbroken by a Settler –
Were all that I could see –
Infinitude – Had'st Thou no Face
That I might look on Thee?

The Silence condescended –
Creation stopped – for Me –
But awed beyond my errand –
I worshipped – did not 'pray' –

Emily Dickinson

Emily Dickinson, an exact contemporary of Christina Rossetti, lived all her life in Amherst, Massachusetts. She is an equally significant religious poet, though her faith was much less conventional than Rossetti's, and eventually she ceased to attend church. This is likely to have been partly a resistance to being told what to believe, and partly her own increasing desire to live an almost completely reclusive life. But, like Rossetti, her apprehension of the natural world, at the cosmic and at the detailed level, is often the arena for her exploration of faith. She was a prolific writer, but very little of her poetry was published during her lifetime, and the exact texts (especially the punctuation) are still disputed today. Like Rossetti, her verses have a surface simplicity, but they have a capacity to open up chasms of meaning for the reader, some of which are alarming. Her sense of the transcendent is powerful, even if its expression is unusual. Again, we have the sense of a remarkably skilled and strong-minded nineteenth-century woman whose religious poetry is an electric blend of passion and constraint.

One of the first things you notice in a poem of Dickinson's is an intriguing entry point and some startling choices of vocabulary. Initially it sounds humdrum, an activity that is part of the speaker's routine. 'My period had come for Prayer –.' But then there is a curious shift, an odd word to use: 'No other Art – would do –.' So, prayer is a kind of 'art'. Does she mean creativity, or skill, or cunning? Do for what? What other 'arts' had she contemplated or tried, or does she just mean she had been putting it off (a not uncommon reaction to the prompt to pray)? Avoidance probably is in the air, since 'My Tactics missed a rudiment', and she then finally addresses

God, who may be responsible both for her urge to pray and her recognition that she cannot avoid it: 'Creator – Was it you?' It remains a question, not an assertion.

The poem continues to subvert religious platitudes, just by using an unexpected choice of vocabulary. 'God grows above.' Grows? Conventional hymnody would say '*dwells* above'. It isn't clear what could be meant by saying that God grows; but perhaps it is an idea transferred from what immediately follows: 'so those who pray/ Horizons – must ascend'. That is, for those who pray, their sense of the presence of God will grow in so far as they are prepared to transcend their normal horizons of vision. The speaker then uses another odd expression, 'so I stepped upon the North'; I suppose this could either mean stepping out into a hilly landscape to get a different perspective on the horizon, or (more likely) imaginatively moved beyond normal religious perception and definitions. And what an unusual name for God, 'this Curious Friend'! It is very different from the tradition of God as divine Lover, perhaps suggesting a sense of detachment as well as affection, but we know that Dickinson rated friendship very highly indeed and felt a powerful loss when one of her friends got married and therefore became much less available.

The next two verses describe the utter absence of reliable signs in the landscape of prayer that could testify to the presence of God. It is a brilliant depiction, in graphic images rooted in the American mid-West, of what other mystics in the apophatic tradition have referred to as the 'cloud of unknowing' or the 'dark night'. Towards every horizon there is simply massive space, without sign of habitation. 'Vast prairies of Air/ Unbroken by a Settler –/ Were all that I could see.' To those of us who have never witnessed the majestic, limitless prairie as far as the eye can see, the image may not quite register in all its power. But then comes the heartfelt actual words of prayer, now directed not to the personal 'Creator' but to this glorious, awesome 'Infinitude': 'Had'st Thou no Face/ That I might look on Thee?'

The poem's speaker is not granted a glimpse of God's face. But the very absence of traditional religious markers nevertheless delivers for her in an extraordinary way, and I do not think this sense of being somehow touched by the transcendent has ever been equalled: 'The Silence condescended –/ Creation stopped – for Me.' The word 'condescended' is exact. Without using tired religious language or calling up extraneous kingly imagery, the verb is perfect to convey the sense that some immense power that is above and beyond her has somehow been willing to grant the speaker a kind of grace and blessing she could not have achieved or even asked for by herself. The apparent 'stopping' of Creation leaves us in a place that is similar to that of John of the Cross at the end of his poem (see p. 128), lost to himself, resting upon his beloved among the lilies. The poem closes with a total redefinition of what prayer means to the speaker. She has been 'awed beyond her errand'; what may have begun as a routine activity or duty has gone utterly beyond these dimensions. She even discards the word 'pray', so far has she moved from the activity of just saying her prayers, or of being the one who initiates the process at all. The word is 'worshipped' – a receptive response of wordless awe.

The Windhover

To Christ our Lord

I caught this morning morning's minion, king-
    dom of daylight's dauphin, dapple-dawn-drawn
      Falcon, in his riding
    Of the rolling underneath him steady air, and
      striding
High there, how he rung upon the rein of a wimpling
    wing
In his ecstasy! then off, off forth on a swing,
    As a skate's heel sweeps smooth on a bow-bend:
      the hurl and gliding
    Rebuffed the big wind. My heart in hiding
Stirred for a bird, – the achieve of, the mastery of the
    thing!

Brute beauty and valour and act, oh, air, pride, plume,
    here
    Buckle! AND the fire that breaks from thee then, a
      billion
Times told lovelier, more dangerous, O my chevalier!

    No wonder of it: shéer plód makes plough down
      sillion
Shine, and blue-bleak embers, ah my dear,
    Fall, gall themselves, and gash gold-vermilion.

Gerard Manley Hopkins

Hopkins was a younger contemporary of Dickinson, and, like her (and indeed like George Herbert), his poems were never published in his lifetime. In Hopkins' case, he may have felt that his passionate absorption in the natural world, and his extraordinary poetic creativity in response to it, may have been distractions from his primary religious vocation as a Roman Catholic priest. He is known to have burned some of his early poetry, but he circulated poems to a few friends, and we are indebted to his friend Robert Bridges for the first collection and publication of Hopkins' work. Like Herbert, the poet seems to have used poetry to explore painstakingly his relationship with God in ways that are occasionally searingly bleak, but at other times resplendent with joy. For someone who feared that he was unlikely to leave a legacy in this world, his innovative experiments with poetic form have had an impact and an influence on subsequent writers like no other.

Though he often wrenches our traditional expectations of English grammar or conventional poetic forms like sonnets, Hopkins was working with a deep knowledge of the traditions he subverted or transformed. He took the time to learn Old English, and its influence can be felt. The serious use of repeated alliteration comes into play, along with the creation of long compound adjectives – a feature of Old English: 'daylight's dauphin, dapple-dawn-drawn Falcon'; 'the rolling underneath him steady air' (the technique of inserting a whole adjectival clause in front of a noun will be used to great effect in later poetry such as that of e. e. cummings).

'The Windhover' is said to have been his favourite poem, and it is the only one that has a dedication below the title: 'To Christ our Lord'. Although the poet frequently shifts between remarkably accurate and detailed depiction of the natural world and some theological theme, this sonnet is an explicit love poem to Christ. And yet it is also all about a kestrel, apparently an actual bird just observed in the early morning – its distinctive flight pattern tackling a powerfully strong wind. In contrast to the previous poem by Emily Dickinson, which ends on a note of ecstatic receptivity ('Creation stopped – for Me –'), Hopkins' poem appears to start with an active achievement on the part of the narrator: 'I caught this morning morning's minion.' And yet it soon becomes clear that the bird has only been 'caught' in the sense that a dedicated birdwatcher means it; the observer has managed to spot the individual bird and follow its distinctive hovering and flight pattern for a while. The first excited sentence tumbles breathlessly over four and half lines of the poem, mimicking the flight path, barely allowing the reader a space to breathe – certainly not at the line endings, until it reaches the word 'ecstasy!'

The exclamation provides a momentary gap while the bird hangs in the air current before making its next sudden swerve: 'then off, off forth on a swing'. It is clear that the bird is riding the wind expertly. Rather than the falcon being blown off course by the weather, the bird is in charge: 'the hurl and gliding/ Rebuffed the big wind'. Watching such mastery of its element, it is clear that what exactly has been 'caught' by the close of the first eight lines of this sonnet is the passion of the narrator: 'My heart in hiding/ Stirred for a bird, – the achieve of, the mastery of the thing!' The poet takes some interesting risks. Rhyming 'Stirred' and 'bird' could sound trite, but it does not; using the verb 'achieve' as a noun to get the right number of syllables in the line could sound odd, but it just seems that the speaker cannot get his words out fast enough to express his excitement. We have a beautiful statement about 'My heart in hiding', which resonates with the mystical language we saw earlier in 'Upon a Gloomy Night' (see p. 127). It has sometimes been said that there is a similarity between the attentive, patient alertness of the birdwatcher and that of the one who seeks to pray.

The sestet of the sonnet starts again, straight in with an attempt to describe the awesome particularity of the falcon and its 'Brute beauty and valour'. A series of single syllable words without grammatical connection follows, as if drawn from the observer as he tries to keep up with the speed of the bird's flight: 'and act, oh, air, pride, plume, here/ Buckle!' The words explode into the beginning of the next line as the bird, full of pride and courage, swerves into yet another unexpected turn. It is at this moment that the focus of the poem itself buckles into a totally different direction, yet one that has been as it were unlocked by the almost visionary joy of watching the bird. A simple, capitalized 'AND' marks the turn (how does Hopkins get away with it?), and suddenly we are into 'the fire that breaks from thee then, a billion/ Times told lovelier, more dangerous'. The one addressed is 'Christ our Lord', and all the knightly vocabulary the poet has been building up in the description of the kestrel ('daylight's dauphin', 'he rung upon the rein', 'valour', 'pride', 'plume') finds its climax in the rather archaic but exactly right synonym for a rather dangerous 'Lord', 'O my chevalier!'

The final three lines are about how the ordinary world of effort and work ('shéer plód') can gleam with beauty. 'Sillion' is an old term revived by Hopkins, meaning the thick, shiny soil turned over by the plough – the same stuff that the little boy stumbles over in Heaney's 'Follower' (see p. 29). Even disappointment ('blue-bleak embers' of a fire) can suddenly break into glory – 'gash gold-vermilion'.

Agnostic

I have lived my life long
With one who cannot speak a word,
Or if a word, not of my tongue
More than sound of stream or bird;
Or if of my tongue, unheard.

I am deaf or this is dumb,
This life and world apart from me
To whom betrothed at birth I came,
In whose silence most I see
A calling soul, calling my scrutiny.

So where deepest silence lies
Gathered to pools, my steps will draw:
The speechless child that sleeps or cries;
Age with the secret, not the power;
The look of utterance on the silent flower.

You with religious faith, to whom
Life speaks in words you understand –
Believe, I also with my dumb
Stranger have made a marriage bond
As strong and deep and torturing and fond.

E. J. Scovell

Scovell was a poet of the twentieth century, born in its first
decade and dying just before the turn of the millennium.

Part of a large rectory family in Sheffield, she grew up in the context of religious faith, but said of herself, 'It seems to me that I realized my agnosticism as soon as I began to question what I was told.' Her poetry tends to be quiet, understated and dealing with careful observations of the natural world or else of intimate domestic matters, especially seen through the eyes of women, and she avoided literary circles. Her work has been underrated compared with her contemporaries, but in spite of her gentle tone there are some steely insights.

Her self-definition as an agnostic, given her upbringing, is likely to be precise. An agnostic is not technically someone who 'doesn't know' whether or not there is a God, but someone who believes that nothing is known, or can be known, about the existence or nature of God. God (if God exists) is not knowable. So there are interesting possibilities of a dialogue between this position and the apophatic mystical tradition which, while profoundly believing in God, holds that God is not knowable or approachable except through love – a love that is prepared to enter a place of 'unknowing': darkness, silence, vast prairies of space.

This poem is fascinating in that it immediately proposes the metaphor of a lifelong relationship with a person to embody the speaker's agnostic faith. It is just that the person is dumb, not just silent, but unable to utter at all: 'I have lived my life long/ With one who cannot speak a word.' But then this assertion is undermined by a caveat: it may be the speaker who doesn't understand the utterance: 'Or if a word, not of my tongue/ More than the sound of stream or bird'. The sounds could be there, but no more interpretable by the human being than any in the natural world. And then this comment is also undermined by another possibility; perhaps the speaker is deaf, rather than the other person dumb or speaking an incomprehensible language: 'Or if of my tongue, unheard'. So straight away we have been given three levels of uncertainty about exactly where the problem of unknowability lies. The stanza is a beautiful demonstration, through its precise hesitancy about what can be asserted, of the experience of being an agnostic.

The second stanza lays bare the problem: 'I am deaf or this is dumb'. The 'other party' in the relationship is 'This life and world apart from me'. Yet it seems that what is a given within the conditions of human existence is not alienation but a sense of connection. The speaker was 'betrothed at birth' to the world outside herself, which seems to call forth her 'scrutiny'. The word suggests deep attentiveness, curiosity and patience. At one level this sounds like a very different calling from that of religious faith, but I wonder. The same sort of thing could be said about prayer, certainly the way Emily Dickinson seems to have understood it. There is a paradox here, which echoes the explorations of the first stanza, as the speaker explains that it is precisely within the experience of silence that she sees 'A calling soul'. She is positively drawn to those aspects of life that seem to contain the most silence.

The third stanza spells out where the 'deepest silence lies' that so attracts her. There are three examples. The first is drawn from the deep relationship with a small child who is pre-language, literally 'speechless'. It is indeed still a mystery how the human child and its first caregivers (usually predominantly the mother) grasp each other's meanings and build together a love which becomes the foundation of the child's personhood. But the poet has picked out those moments which are the most mysterious, when the child cries for unknown reasons or when it is asleep. (Compare Scovell's poem discussed earlier, 'Child Waking' (p. 13), which targets the precise moment between sleep and waking when the 'soul' may perhaps be open to scrutiny.) The second example is that of very old age, which may have declined (or progressed) to a stage beyond that of ordinary language: 'Age with the secret, not the power'. This is someone who has spent time with a group of largely helpless people often written off by society, but who perhaps know something, as death approaches, which they will never be able to communicate to the rest of us. And finally the beauty and inscrutability of the natural world that so moves us: 'The look of utterance on the silent flower'. Does it have something to say to us if it could, or not?

And then the speaker addresses those who seem to have a certainty of belief not open to her. She does not deny their lived experience but she vigorously rejects any sense of superiority they may claim over her, deaf or uncomprehending as she may be, and her protest has an edge of anger: 'You with religious faith, to whom/ Life speaks in words you understand'. And the next line explodes on its first word, 'Believe'. They are adept at belief, well, they can do her the courtesy in return of believing in the authenticity of her experience of agnostic faith. 'I also with my dumb/ Stranger have made a marriage bond.' I can't help comparing Scovell's 'dumb stranger' with Dickinson's 'Curious Friend'. Both are fascinating, personal images of whatever transcendent presence may be out there. Equally fascinating is the image of 'marriage', and the unforgettable four adjectives with which the poem ends demonstrate a deep inward grasp of both the spiritual quest and the nature of marriage, with its tenacious connectedness and inescapable ambivalences: 'As strong and deep and torturing and fond'.

Tidal

The waves run up the shore
and fall back. I run
up the approaches of God
and fall back. The breakers return
reaching a little further,
gnawing away at the main land.
They have done this thousands
of years, exposing little by little
the rock under the soil's face.
I must imitate them only
in my return to the assault,
not in their violence. Dashing
my prayers at him will achieve
little other than the exposure
of the rock under his surface.
My returns must be made
on my knees. Let despair be known
as my ebb-tide; but let prayer
have its springs, too, brimming,
disarming him; discovering somewhere
among his fissures deposits of mercy
where trust may take root and grow.

R. S. Thomas

R. S. Thomas was an almost exact contemporary of E. J.
Scovell and, like her, wrote and published continuously over a
long lifetime. He was born in Cardiff and his mother tongue

was English; he did not learn Welsh until he was 30, which meant that he felt that was too late for him to be able to write poetry in Welsh. He is widely regarded as the foremost Welsh poet writing in English in the twentieth century. Thomas was ordained as a priest in the Church in Wales as a young man, and served in six different rural communities. Much of his early poetry reflects the nature of his parishioners, and he presents the hardship of their lives as farmers in a rugged and unyielding landscape entirely without sentimentality. His later poetry focuses a good deal on the inward struggles of the religious life, particularly the difficulty of prayer, and he stands out among his contemporaries as a poet of inter-national stature who seriously wrestled with God.

Christians who experience prayer as a challenge can find the comfort of knowing that the poet has been there before them. The problem of whether or not God is listening, or indeed is even there at all, is repeatedly explored. There are poems in which the speaker is fruitlessly wearing out his knees in a cold rural church; or finding that he is stuck in the church porch, unable to fully enter but equally unable simply to leave. Sometimes prayer is likened to that sense that the absence in the room is that of someone who has just departed; sometimes it is like flinging little stones at an upper window in order to get someone to wake up – was that or was it not a twitch of the curtain? You have the feeling that the speaker in Thomas's poems are nothing at all like the believers referred to in Scovell's poem, to whom 'Life speaks in words you understand'. Any sense of God's presence with the one who prays seems to be desperately hard won, if at all, and yet he persists. In this poem the overriding metaphor is taken from observation of the restless action of the tides on the coast of the North Wales Llyn peninsula where Thomas lived.

'The waves run up the shore/ and fall back. I run/ up the approaches of God/ and fall back.' This simple analogy is stated in repetitive terms, so that the phrase 'and fall back' is emphasized at the start of a line. Of course this echoes exactly what the pattern of the waves does, over and over; but it also introduces the sense of helpless retreat which accompanies any effort to pray. Any momentary success in approaching God is immediately paralleled by withdrawal. (Compare the Song of Songs (see p. 123), where the lover seems to withdraw as soon as he is approached.) But the waves of the sea do progress a little, 'reaching a little further' when they return – both because this is an incoming tide and because coastal erosion means that the sea literally gets fractionally further in as it encroaches on the shore, 'gnawing away at the main land'. This is an accurate observation about that coastline, where the sea has indeed been 'exposing little by little/ the rock under the soil's face'. But it is interesting to reflect on what it might mean to be 'gnawing away' at God or God's defences. This is a disturbing image.

It seems that the poem's speaker wants to retreat from the metaphor, perhaps because he senses the darkness of it. However, in apparently wanting to choose only one aspect of the analogy to mirror, he beds in our awareness of how potentially aggressive it is to describe prayer in this way. In selecting only the waves' 'return', the poet manages to mention again their 'violence', and to describe his own behaviour as a kind of 'assault', 'Dashing/ my prayers at him'. Thomas is not a poet who uses extra words or would fail to notice any underlying menace in the words he chooses. So we are to understand that, for all his intention to approach God gently, this is not what is happening in his prayer. There is a kind of desperation here, which is expressed in the image of the kind of waves that crash on to the shore and then are sucked back fiercely, revealing bare rocks that have been scoured of sand or soil or clinging plants. A battery of prayer only succeeds in exposing a hard and unyielding God. We are in the realm of Donne's self-destructive sonnet (see p. 137).

'My returns must be made/ on my knees.' A quite different demeanour is required, reminiscent of the ancient tradition of pilgrimage, where part of a penitential journey is to be made on one's knees. And now, the speaker of the poem does subtly change the mood, while still pursuing the tidal imagery. The despair that underlay a desperate sort of dashing at God is now to be defined 'as my ebb-tide', the periodic withdrawal of the sea's approach. But he prays, 'let prayer/ have its springs, too, brimming,/ disarming him'. This is the spring tide, when the high-tide level goes much further than normal, and of course would wholly cover the rocks that are normally exposed. The repeated 'ing' sound in the verbs reinforces the word 'springs' – which also implies that equinoxial season of growth when indeed the tides are at their highest. Now there is no 'gnawing away' but a full embrace of the land by the sea. And in the 'fissures' of God small plants of trust and hope may get a foothold.

Mary an Elizabeth

An dey hüld ticht ta een anidder
stumsed bi happenstance, da
chancy gaets der lives wis taen
but nivver o der ain choosin.
A quickenin for da aalder cousin,
barren as Judah's heichts dey said.
Foo her heart was tiftit at skirlin
infants, da smeegs o smug weemen;
wis scordit bi da skyimp o matrons.

Mary, aa but a bairn herself,
salistit at da feel o kindly airms
aroond her, der swallin wames
atween dem; awa fae da clash
an do een o bawdy men, dem at
ogled her but caad her a hoor,
a hussy, a limmer. Shö keepit
her coonsil aboot dis sainin,
o finnin favour among weemen.

But for noo der glaikit men wis
i da grip o angels, dumb-struck wi
messages; steelin demsels fornenst
nods an winks, da coorse tongues
o street an market-place; glufft
bi dis queer an silent ontack;
o der place I da lives o men
untimely boarn; men wi speerit
ta turn der peerie worlds headicraa.

And they held tight to one another
bewildered by happenstance, the
chancy paths their lives were taking
but never of their own choosing.
A quickening for the older cousin,
barren as Judah's heights they said.
How her heart had throbbed at laughing
infants, the smirks of smug women;
was slashed by the mockery of matrons.

Mary, still but a bairn herself,
relaxed at the feel of kindly arms
around her, their swelling wombs
between them, away from the gossip
and the eyes of bawdy men, those who
ogled her but called her a whore,
a hussy, a temptress. She kept
her counsel about this blessing,
of finding favour among women.

But for now their giddy men were
in the grip of angels, dumb-struck with
messages; steeling themselves against
nods and winks, the coarse tongues
of street and market-place; scared
by this strange and silent drama;
of their place in the lives of men
untimely born; men with the spirit
to turn their little worlds upside down.

Christine De Luca

The last two poems of this section are by poets who are still writing. Both of them have addressed religious themes, and these poems are examples of how contemporary writers may 'tell it slant', when it comes to expressing the mystery of God's love for humanity, and quite what the tremendous consequences may be in the lives of individuals who have said 'yes' to that love. These poets engage with the major Christian doctrines of incarnation and resurrection, but do it via the impact of such mysteries on the ordinary characters in the story of salvation. At one level this is profoundly traditional. The Gospel writers work primarily with skilfully told stories, rather than theological arguments. And over the centuries, Christians have meditated using the technique of *lectio divina*, which emphasizes seeking to inhabit the biblical story using imagination and empathy, to 'be present' oneself in the narrative. To be a Christian believer is not so much about assenting to a series of doctrinal statements, as it is agreeing to place oneself inside the story, which then transforms how the whole world appears. And yet I think it is also true that contemporary religious poets, rather than addressing God directly, may find it more appealing to write from inside the biblical story, letting the confusion and uncertainty the characters experience in encountering God stand for our own. Responding to God is not straightforward, and to do so has an impact on the relationships between people, drawing them together but also setting them apart from others who are outside the experience.

Christine De Luca writes in both English and Shetlandic. There is dispute whether the latter is a dialect of Scots or a separate language, but it has maintained a high degree of autonomy because of the isolation of the Shetland Isles from mainland Scotland. It has a good deal of unique vocabulary and some Norwegian influence. But readers of English will find that they can appreciate this poem in Shetlandic, if they are helped with a transliteration of the spelling, and an explanation of particular vocabulary. (It helps to speak it out loud.) It enables us to hear the story afresh, with blunt and colloquial voices commenting on what happens.

'Mary an Elizabeth' celebrates Luke's story of the 'visitation'. He first tells of the miraculous conception of John the Baptist to Elizabeth, a relative of Mary's. Then within the story of John, in the sixth month of Elizabeth's pregnancy, he sets the account of Jesus' conception, after Mary has given her consent to the angel of the annunciation. Mary travels to visit her cousin and, as they greet each other, Elizabeth feels the baby move in her womb (the 'quickening', which used to be thought to be the moment when a child's soul was bestowed). Mary is then shown singing the great anthem of the Magnificat, with its promise of a world turned upside down – the rich brought low and the poor lifted high (Luke 1.46).

Assuming the reader is familiar with this background, the poem starts with the classic moment of the women's embrace, frequently depicted in religious art: 'An dey hüld ticht ta een anidder'. It is as if they have just fallen into each other's arms. They are not just female relatives who have chanced to become pregnant at the same time. They are the only people who can grasp what is going on for each other; both have been gripped by the Holy Spirit in ways that will utterly change their lives. Both of them understand being the object of scorn: Elizabeth because her barrenness up to this point has made her the object of 'da smeegs o smug weemen', and Mary because she has agreed to become pregnant without a husband.

The next stanza emphasizes Mary's youth, 'aa but a bairn herself', and allows her to relax in her cousin's 'kindly airms'. There is the lovely detail that she can also feel 'der swallin wames/ atween dem'. In the centre of the poem is a place of refuge from the scandal her condition has given rise to. We can hear the tones of the men who troll her while openly lusting after her, 'dem at/ ogled her but caad her a hoor'. And the attitude of their womenfolk is conveyed by an ironic subversion of the words of the angel, who declared: 'Blessed art thou among women'. Mary kept her mouth shut about whether the women themselves agreed with that. And the fact is that the two women's 'glaikit men' were neither use nor comfort in this situation: bedazzled by angels themselves (Luke 1.5–23 and Matthew 1.18–25) and hyper-sensitive to 'da coorse tongues/ o street an market-place'.

So, while it barely mentions God, the poem depicts with humour and bluntness the impact of God's actions in entering the world of humanity, justifying that wonderful word 'headicraa' as the world is turned upside down.

Emmaus

First the sun, then the shadow,
so that I screw my eyes to see
my friend's face, and its lines seem
different, and the voice shakes in the hot air.
Out of the rising white dust, feet
tread a shape, and, out of step,
another flat sound, stamped between voice
and ears, dancing in the gaps, and dodging
where words and feet do not fall.

When our eyes meet, I see bewilderment
(like mine); we cannot learn
the rhythm we are asked to walk,
and what we hear is not each other.
Between us is filled up, the silence
is filled up, lines of our hands
and faces pushed into shape
by the solid stranger, and the static
breaks up our waves like dropped stones.

So it is necessary to carry him with us,
cupped between hands and profiles,
so that the table is filled up, and as
the food is set and the first wine splashes,
a solid thumb and finger tear the thunderous
grey bread. Now it is cold, even indoors,
and the light falls sharply on our bones;

the rain breathes out hard, dust blackens,
and our released voices shine with water.

Rowan Williams

Rowan Williams, former Archbishop of Canterbury, once remarked: 'I dislike the idea of being a religious poet. I would prefer to be a poet for whom religious things mattered intensely.'[12] Here, like Christine De Luca, he takes a famous biblical narrative and inhabits it from the inside. The speaker in the poem is one of the characters (perhaps Cleopas) in the story of the journey to Emmaus (Luke 24.13), who, after the catastrophe of Jesus' execution on a Roman cross, walks from Jerusalem with his companion, discussing all the terrible events that have taken place, destroying all the disciples' hopes. After a while, they are joined by another traveller, who gets involved in the discussion and starts pointing out how all this was foretold by Scripture. On arrival at Emmaus, the stranger is invited in for a meal, and as he breaks the bread is suddenly recognized as being Jesus himself, sitting between them. The companions immediately run back to the city to announce that Jesus is alive, just as the women of their company had already said. It is a classic 'resurrection' narrative: what happens is unexpected, challenging to the people involved, and actually rather troubling. Their eyes are 'held' so that they are initially unable to recognize Jesus' presence; their demeanour is depressed; they are engaged in trying to return to normality, an effort that is overturned by his appearance, but only in retrospect can they interpret what just happened. ('Did not our hearts burn within us when he expounded the scriptures?')

By his title, Williams calls up this story in the reader's mind and immediately places us within the consciousness of one of the travellers, as he walks home on a dusty and hot afternoon. The first line evokes the strong contrast between the slanting sunlight and the shadows this casts, but also implies the tragedy that has overwhelmed those involved in Jesus' story: 'First the sun, then the shadow'. The tricky light seems to be what makes the speaker have to screw his eyes, and then what makes his friend's face look different. We are conscious of searing, disorienting heat ('hot air', 'rising white dust'). Then there seems to be another footfall, 'out of step' with the companions as they walk and converse: a 'shape', a 'flat sound', which is 'dancing in the gaps, and dodging/ where words and feet do not fall'. A mysterious new presence is hinted at, and it is disconcerting. This depiction of the event is reminiscent of T. S. Eliot's *The Waste Land*, in 'What the Thunder said', which asks about the unseen other 'who walks always beside you'.[13]

The second stanza expresses this bewilderment. The travellers manage to look one another in the eye, but something seems to have completely shifted how they are relating to one another. Their steps are now out of kilter, and, like clumsy beginners on a dance floor, they can't seem to learn how to move in the rhythm they now need to keep. Their conversation has been disrupted, 'and what we hear is not each other'. The presence that has come between them is not quite visible, but it seems to be very insistent, permeating every possible space between the travellers: 'Between us is filled up, the silence/ is filled up'. And the presence seems to have a concrete reality which is greater than their own, so powerful that its pressure reshapes their boundaries: 'lines of our hands/

and faces pushed into shape/ by the solid stranger'. This is a wonderful, experimental way of suggesting the nature of resurrection reality: as something that cannot quite be pinned down, is not immediately recognizable, and yet transforms everything within and between the witnesses of it. The implication is that this is true, not just for this encounter but for those who encounter the risen Christ throughout time.

The final stanza, with its arrival at the place where, effectively, the first post-resurrection Eucharist will be enacted, makes clear that Christ is precisely experienced *between* his friends: 'So it is necessary to carry him with us.' It is interesting to notice how an elusive presence that so far has not exactly seemed to have a bodily form can now be 'cupped between hands and profiles', and fill up a table setting. And, as the physical elements of hospitality and nourishment are introduced and their solidity emphasized ('the food is set and the first wine splashes'), the bodily presence of Jesus is suddenly noticed and he is evanescent no longer: 'a solid thumb and finger tear the thunderous/ grey bread'. As his recognizable hand grasps the very ordinary bread, his identity is simultaneously grasped by his friends. The word 'thunderous' is interesting. To describe bread, it sounds dauntingly heavy and chewy (though undoubtedly absolutely real). In terms of the tone and significance of the shared encounter, 'thunderous' suggests something rather too frighteningly real. But also, in the context of the searing heat of the journey, the prospect of imminent rain is a relief. And this is where the poem ends, with the blessing of rain in a hot climate. It is a detail introduced by the poet (perhaps another echo of *The Waste Land*, where, at the end, thunder implies some hope of healing). It symbolizes the moment of recognition at the return of love, where the friends of Jesus are freed from grief and bewilderment, and their 'released voices shine with water.'

Postscript

The Great Lover

I have been so great a lover: filled my days
So proudly with the splendour of Love's praise,
The pain, the calm, and the astonishment,
Desire illimitable, and still content,
And all dear names men use, to cheat despair,
For the perplexed and viewless streams that bear
Our hearts at random down the dark of life . . .
These I have loved:
          White plates and cups, clean-gleaming,
Ringed with blue lines; and feathery, faery dust;
Wet roofs, beneath the lamp-light; the strong crust
Of friendly bread; and many-tasting food;
Rainbows; and the blue bitter smoke of wood;
And radiant raindrops couching in cool flowers;
And flowers themselves, that sway through sunny
          hours,
Dreaming of moths that drink them under the moon;
Then, the cool kindliness of sheets, that soon
Smooth away trouble; and the rough male kiss
Of blankets; grainy wood; live hair that is
Shining and free; blue-massing clouds; the keen
Unpassioned beauty of a great machine;
The benison of hot water; furs to touch;
The good smell of old clothes; and others such –

The comfortable smell of friendly fingers,
Hair's fragrance, and the musty reek that lingers
About dead leaves and last year's ferns . . .

                                       Dear names,
And thousand other throng to me! Royal flames;
Sweet water's dimpling laugh from tap or spring;
Holes in the ground; and voices that do sing;
Voices in laughter, too; and body's pain,
Soon turned to peace; and the deep-panting train;
Firm sands; the little dulling edge of foam
That browns and dwindles as the wave goes home;
And washen stones, gay for an hour; the cold
Graveness of iron; moist black earthen mould;
Sleep; and high places; footprints in the dew;
And oaks; and brown horse-chestnuts, glossy-new;
And new-peeled sticks; and shining pools on grass; –
All these have been my loves. And these shall pass . . .

Rupert Brooke

This brief postscript contains two works, separated by two millennia, about the nature of love. This poem from the early twentieth century is focused on the experience and practice of all kinds of love in this beautiful, passing world: the second, taken from the first-century letters of Paul of Tarsus, speaks of the capacity of love to last eternally, when nothing else does.

I have shortened Rupert Brooke's poem by taking out a total of about thirty-six lines in two places: after 'down the dark of life', and then at the end, after 'and these shall pass'. This is partly because this anthology needed reasonably brief poems, but also because I think the edit highlights what the contemporary reader responds most strongly to (visceral, concrete word pictures, presented with humour and delight) and removes what we tend to like less (a certain wordy sententiousness). But of course this may reflect simply my own prejudices. At the start of the twentieth century, we see in this poem the movement that was beginning to happen across many parts of the culture, where the mundane and the everyday was seen afresh as the locus of a rich reality, suitable for depiction and contemplation by poets and artists just for their own sake, unadorned by symbolism, abstraction or romantic soft focusing.

The poem begins with a wonderful joke on the concept of being, or aspiring to be, a 'great lover'. It seems to be a classical paean to 'the splendour of Love's praise' in the abstract (note the capitalization which traditionally denotes a god, whether classical or Christian). We seem to be solidly within the domain of Eros, for what follows is a series of contrasting features of the experience of love that seems to witness to that volatile god's presence: 'pain', 'calm', 'astonishment', 'Desire illimitable, and still content'. Romantic love seems to be invoked in rather the same way as it is at the end of Matthew Arnold's 'Dover Beach', as the only force that can overcome existential meaninglessness and 'cheat despair,/ For the perplexed and viewless streams that bear/ Our hearts at random down the dark of life'. But then there is the utterly arresting 'turn': 'These I have loved:/ White plates and cups, clean-gleaming,/ Ringed with blue lines.' We all absolutely recognize those traditional pieces of everyday crockery, but we weren't expecting their arrival in a poem about love's splendour.

The list that follows is a fascinating mixture of objects or plain food from daily life, mingled with observations from the natural world and typically mixed British weather, along with hints of human romantic encounters. Sometimes the details sound rather romanticized, like the 'radiant raindrops couching in cool flowers', but then the list encompasses quite different things like 'the keen/ Unpassioned beauty of a great machine', or simply 'Holes in the ground'. There is throughout a sense of delight and contentment experienced in the details of living, so that for instance a loaf of bread seems itself to be a source of strength and comfort: 'the strong crust/ Of friendly bread'; and getting into bed is to find oneself embraced by 'the cool kindliness of sheets'. However, the corresponding reference to the 'rough male kiss/ Of blankets', while absolutely accurate about the scratchiness of those heavy grey woollen blankets that were a feature of early twentieth-century life, startlingly introduces the distinct impression of a kiss from a man with a stubbly chin.

It is noticeable how many senses are invoked by this poem's list of love objects: touch ('The benison of hot water; furs to touch', 'Firm sands'); sight ('live hair that is/ Shining and free', 'blue-massing clouds', 'washen stones, gay for an hour'); hearing ('Sweet water's dimpling laugh', 'the deep-panting train'); smell ('The good smell of old clothes . . . friendly fingers,/ Hair's fragrance', 'the musty reek that lingers/ About dead leaves'). The sheer diversity of what this narrator has loved makes you feel that the list is almost random; it is not so much about selecting his favourite things as implying that living itself, with an open heart, constantly provides material for delight. This is the case whether one encounters classically beautiful scenes like rainbows or 'shining pools on grass', or just the 'little dulling edge of foam/ That browns and dwindles as the wave goes home'. Even 'the body's pain' itself can be a source of comfort, as you notice when it is 'Soon turned to peace'. What counts is to keep the senses awake and notice the details of daily life, all of which can be delighted in and loved. The poignant truth is that this is the reality of the world we inhabit, and everything (including ourselves) is mortal. On the cusp of the First World War (the poet died in 1915) he declares: 'All these have been my loves. And these shall pass . . .'

1 Corinthians 13

I may speak in tongues –
human speech or the language of angels –
but if I have no love,
I am an echoing gong or a loud-wailing cymbal.
And if I have the gift of speaking God's inspired word,
and can grasp all mysteries and all secret knowledge,
and if I have all faith, so as to move mountains,
but if I have no love, I am nothing.
And if I give away all my resources to feed others,
and if I devote my whole life to an impressive cause,
but if I have no love, it benefits me nothing.

Love is patient, love is kind:
not envious, or boastful, or full of its own importance;
it does not behave dishonourably,
or strive for its own advantage;
it does not get irritable;
it does not brood over injuries;
it does not rejoice in wrongdoing,
but rejoices with others in the truth.
It endures all things, it has faith in all things,
it hopes all things, it perseveres in all things.

Love never falls away.
As for inspired words, they will come to nothing.
As for tongues, they will fall silent.
As for secret knowledge, it will be superseded.
For we know only in part and prophesy only in part,

but when completeness comes, what is partial will be
    superseded.
When I was a child, I spoke as a child;
I thought like a child, I reasoned like a child.
Now I am an adult, I have done with childishness.
For now we see indistinctly in a dark mirror.
But then, face to face.
Now I understand only in part, then I shall
    understand fully,
even as I have been fully understood.
And now, what remains is faith, hope, love, these
    three.
And the greatest of these is love.

Editor's translation

The traditional version of this chapter of Paul's letter to the Corinthians is very well known, as it is often chosen as a wedding reading. Although it is not an example of classical Greek poetry (which operated through a strict metre), the chapter is certainly a rhetorical set piece, patterned and structured in a way that would render it recognizably 'poetic' in our contemporary culture. I have placed it as the last poem in this book because it is a highly influential text, and it attempts to sum up the nature of love's importance in human experience, identity and ultimate aspiration. In Greek there are several words for 'love'; the term used here is *agape*, that is, not the same as erotic or familial love, but a wider concept which early Christians seem to have seized on as distinctively their own.

In undertaking a translation, I found that the chapter naturally falls into three parts, like stanzas. In the first section, the author asserts that every sort of impressive contemporary religious practice (whether Christian or pagan) is completely irrelevant if it is not accompanied by love. The list begins with 'tongues', and the same word can mean both ordinary languages and the phenomenon of 'speaking in tongues', which is still practised in some churches today, and which Paul may be referring to in his previous chapter (1 Corinthians 12.10). This may be what he means by 'the language of angels', and it is both beautiful and impressive. The 'loud-wailing' cymbal is one that is not just noisy, but redolent of the sound of mourning, the speechless cry heard at funerals. 'Speaking God's inspired word' is how I have rendered what is often rendered 'prophecies' – not predictions but intelligible discernment about God's message here and now. 'Mysteries and all secret knowledge' refer to the many Gnostic cults that flourished in the time of Paul; they offered initiates a sense of belonging to an elite. Donating possessions is a Christian practice attested in the Acts of the Apostles; for a time, there seems to have been a practice of holding all goods in common among Christians, and retaining private wealth was frowned on (Acts 2.45). The line about 'an impressive cause' is my attempt to render a clause that is difficult because there are various versions of it in the sources. One version is literally 'though I deliver my body to be burned', but most scholars think the better version is 'so that I may boast'. We can see why the former rendering was so meaningful in the era when English translations of the Bible were a controversial innovation and some people did actually go to the stake for their faith. But we can see that the underlying principle is still that you could go to extremes in your sacrificial religiosity, but still have missed the point if you lack love.

The second stanza describes how love behaves, and what it does not do. This is in contrast to our contemporary interest in how love feels. This section is undoubtedly the reason why the reading is considered ideal for weddings. While not explicitly addressed to romantic situations, the detailed and practical advice is excellent if followed for avoiding or resolving domestic conflict and preserving lifelong respect and mutual support. Paul's own initial audience was a community that was riven by competitive cliques that failed to respect each other's sensitivities and differing social power and wealth.

The final section is visionary, exploring why it is that love remains, even when all else fails or falls away. It returns to the impressive religious practices of the opening stanza: prophecies, tongues and secret knowledge. All of these are but partial glimpses into the nature of divine reality, and all of them will be subsumed into 'completeness'. Paul seems to have believed that the 'end times' would happen in his own lifetime, and that God's completeness would 'come' in some glorious way that we cannot fully describe or anticipate. His analogy is that of being a child and then becoming an adult. However much a child yearns to grow up, there is a good deal about adult life that cannot be understood until you reach that point. The next analogy is that of looking into a mirror – seeing 'in a glass darkly' in the traditional phrase. Mirrors in Paul's time were not, like ours, made of silvered glass reflecting a clear image. They were polished metal, offering a hazy reflection indeed. The contrast with 'face to face' is huge; but it is that intimate vision which explains why love is eternally valid, when everything else falls away. We were created by love; we have grown and developed under love's gaze; we find our greatest joy in surrendering to that love and being capable of returning that gaze, fully accepted, fully known, fully understood.

Notes

1 Rowan Williams, *Ponder These Things* (London: Canterbury Press, 2002).

2 Williams, *Ponder These Things*.

3 Williams, *Ponder These Things*.

4 Neil Astley (ed.), *Bedouin of the London Evening: Collected Poems of Rosemary Tonks* (Hexham: Bloodaxe Books, 2014).

5 Daisy Goodwin, *Poems to Last a Lifetime* (London: HarperCollins, 2004).

6 Sonnet 130.

7 Imtiaz Dharker, 'Talking about Shakespeare', a talk given at the Hay Festival, 2016.

8 From the programme *Cornwall's Native Poet: Charles Causley*, broadcast on BBC 4, 22 October 2018.

9 Don Paterson, *Reading Shakespeare's Sonnets* (London: Faber and Faber, 2010).

10 W. H. Auden, 'Funeral Blues', *Collected Poems* (London: Faber and Faber, 1976).

11 Letter from Christina Rossetti to Edmund Gosse, 26 March 1884.

12 Rowan Williams, *The Poems of Rowan Williams* (Oxford: Perpetua Press, 2002).

13 T. S. Eliot, *The Waste Land* (London: Faber and Faber, 1954).

Acknowledgements

Thanks to Dr Jill Robson, who read and commented on my manuscript.

The publisher and author acknowledge with thanks permission to reproduce extracts from the following.

Every effort has been made to acknowledge fully the sources of material reproduced in this book. The publisher apologizes for any omissions that may remain and, if notified, will ensure that full acknowledgements are made in a subsequent edition.

W. H. Auden, 'The More Loving One', from *Selected Poems*, Faber & Faber, 1979. Copyright © 1934 by W. H. Auden, renewed 2007. Reprinted by permission of Curtis Brown, Ltd.

Charles Causley, 'Angel Hill', from *Collected Poems 1951–2000*, Picador, 2000. Used by permission of David Higham Associates.

Gillian Clarke, 'Baby-Sitting', from *Selected Poems*, Carcanet Press, 1985. Used by permission of Carcanet Press Limited.

Christine De Luca, 'Mary an Elizabeth'. Used by permission of Christine De Luca.

Christine De Luca, 'What's in a name?', from *Dat Trickster Sun: Poems*, Mariscat Press, 2014. Used by permission of Christine De Luca.

Imtiaz Dharker, 'The trick', from *Luck Is the Hook*, Bloodaxe, 2018. Used by permission of Bloodaxe.

Emily Dickinson, 'My period had come for Prayer', from *The Poems of Emily Dickinson: Variorum Edition*, edited by Ralph W. Franklin, Cambridge, Mass.: The Belknap Press of Harvard University Press, Copyright © 1998 by the President and Fellows of Harvard College. Copyright © 1951, 1955 by the President and Fellows of Harvard College. Copyright © renewed 1979, 1983 by the President and Fellows of Harvard College. Copyright © 1914, 1918, 1919, 1924, 1929, 1930, 1932, 1935, 1937, 1942 by Martha Dickinson Bianchi. Copyright © 1952, 1957, 1958, 1963, 1965 by Mary L. Hampson.

Carol Ann Duffy, 'River', from *Rapture*. Published by Picador, 2015. Copyright © Carol Ann Duffy. Reproduced by permission of the author c/o Rogers, Coleridge & White Ltd, 20 Powis Mews, London W11 1JN.

Ruth Fainlight, 'Handbag', from *New and Collected Poems*, Bloodaxe, 2010. Used by permission of Bloodaxe.

U. A. Fanthorpe, 'Atlas', from *New and Collected Poems*, Enitharmon, 2010. Used by permission of Dr R. V. Bailey.

Seamus Heaney, 'Follower' and 'Scaffolding', from *100 Poems*, Faber & Faber, 2018. Used by permission of Faber & Faber Ltd.

Ted Hughes, 'Bride and Groom Lie Hidden for Three Days', from *New and Selected Poems 1957–1994*, Faber & Faber, 1995. Used by permission of Faber & Faber Ltd.

Jane Kenyon, 'Staying at Grandma's', from *Collected Poems*. Copyright © 2005 by The Estate of Jane Kenyon. Reprinted with the permission of The Permissions Company, Inc, on behalf of Graywolf Press, <www.graywolfpress.org>.

Edwin Morgan, 'Strawberries', from *Collected Poems 1949–1987*, Carcanet Press, 1990 (from *The Second Life*, 1968). Used by permission of Carcanet Press Limited.

Sinéad Morrissey, 'The Rope', from *On Balance*, Carcanet Press, 2017. Used by permission of Carcanet Press Limited.

Sylvia Plath, 'Morning Song, from *The Collected Poems of Sylvia Plath*, edited by Ted Hughes. Copyright © 1960, 1965, 1971, 1981 by the Estate of Sylvia Plath. Editorial material copyright © 1981 by Ted Hughes. Reprinted by permission of HarperCollins Publishers.

Siegfried Sassoon, 'Slumber-Song', from *Selected Poems*, Faber & Faber, 1968. Used by permission of Barbara Levy Literary Agency.

E. J. Scovell, 'Agnostic' and 'Child Waking', from *Selected Poems of E. J. Scovell*, Carcanet Press, 1991. Used by permission of Carcanet Press Limited.

Rosemary Tonks, 'Story of a Hotel Room', from *Bedouin of the London Evening*, Bloodaxe, 2014. Used by permission of Bloodaxe.

Rowan Williams, 'Emmaus', from *Headwaters*, Perpetua/Carcanet Press, 2008. Used by permission of Carcanet Press Limited.

Rowan Williams, 'Our Lady of Vladimir', from *After Silent Centuries*, Carcanet Press, 1994. Used by permission of Carcanet Press Limited.